Math
KS2-Year 3/4/5

Multiplication And Division
Addition, Subtraction, Word problems, Fractions

William. Education

Activity books to help children progress through each phase of their learning.

Don't hesitate to give your opinion (constructive ;-)) and your ideas for improvement after your purchase, because I really want to offer quality, Have fun.

Peaperback ASIN : 9798859406036

Copyright ©2023 By William. Education
All Rights Reserved

No part of this book may be used or reproduced by any means, graphic, electronic, or mechanical, including photocopying, recording, taping, or by any information storage retrieval system without the written permission of the publisher except in the case of brief quotations embodied in critical articles and reviews

TABLE OF CONTENTS

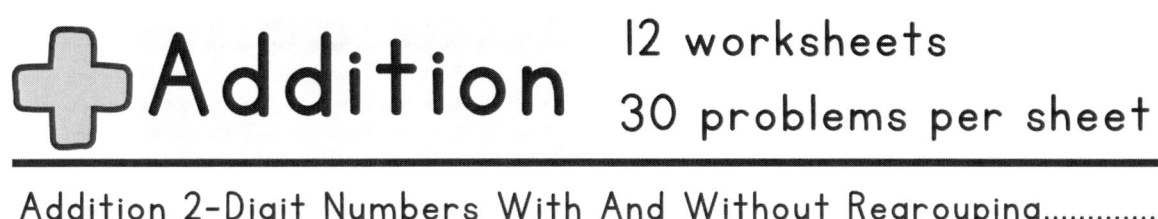

Addition
12 worksheets
30 problems per sheet

Addition 2-Digit Numbers With And Without Regrouping.....................01-04
Addition 3-Digit Numbers With And Without Regrouping.....................05-08
Addition 4-Digit Numbers With And Without Regrouping.....................09-12

Subtraction
12 worksheets
30 problems per sheet

Subtraction 2-Digit Numbers Without Borrowing 13-16
Subtraction 3-Digit Numbers With Borrowing 17-20
Subtraction 4-Digit Numbers Without Borrowing 21-24

Multiplication
12 worksheets
30 problems per sheet

Multiplication, 2-digit by 1-digit numbers..25-28
Multiplication, 2-digit by 2-digit numbers..29-32
Multiplication, 3-digit by 3-digit numbers..33-36

Division
15 worksheets
40 problems per sheet

Division, 2-digit by 1-digit numbers 37-40
Division, 3-digit by 1-digit numbers 41-44
Division, 3-digit by 2-digit numbers..45-48
Division, 4-digit by 2-digit numbers..49-51

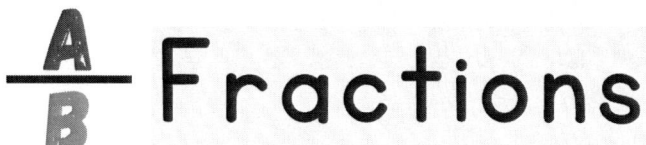 **Fractions**   12 worksheets
40 problems per sheet

Adding Fractions..52-54
Subtracting Fractions...55-57
Multiplying Fractions...58-60
Dividing Fractions..61-63

Word Problems   12 worksheets
10 problems per sheet

Word Problems... 64-75

Solutions to the exercises can be found in the back of the book

Addition ✚

---

12 worksheets
30 problems per sheet

William. Education

Examples

Example 1 (2-digit numbers)

①
```
  98
+ 63
-----
```

②
```
   1
  98
+ 63
-----
   1
```

③
```
   1
  98
+ 63
-----
 161
```

Example 2 (3-digit numbers)

①
```
  286
+  82
-----
```

②
```
  286
+  82
-----
    8
```

③
```
   1
  286
+  82
-----
   68
```

④
```
   1
  286
+  82
-----
  368
```

Example 3 (3-digit numbers)

①
```
  387
+ 688
-----
```

②
```
    1
  387
+ 688
-----
    5
```

③
```
   1 1
  387
+ 688
-----
   75
```

④
```
   1 1
  387
+ 688
-----
 1075
```

Example 4 (2-digit numbers)

```
  ¹87      ¹95       24      ¹81       82
+ 88     + 38     + 25     + 49     + 74
 ───      ───      ───      ───      ───
 175      133       49      130      156

   32       83       50      ¹16      ¹48
+  19     + 36     + 40     + 18     + 23
  ───      ───      ───      ───      ───
   51      119       90       34       71
```

Example 5 (3-digit numbers)

```
  ¹¹487     ¹¹557      721     ¹¹989     ¹¹453
+   778   +   868   +  975   +    54   +    49
  ─────    ─────    ─────    ─────    ─────
   1265     1425     1696     1043      502

  ¹¹675      ¹454      621      101     ¹¹538
+   569   +   929   +  747   +  661   +   783
  ─────    ─────    ─────    ─────    ─────
   1244     1383     1368      762     1321
```

Example 6 (4-digit numbers)

```
  ¹2168    ¹¹4876     ¹7284     3753    ¹¹¹4449
+  1080   +  8143   +  7323   +  244   +   855
  ─────    ─────    ─────    ─────     ─────
   3248    13019    14607     3997      5304

 ¹¹5278    ¹7681     4572     7360     ¹8270
+  1572   +  9247   +  7323   +  535   +  384
  ─────    ─────    ─────    ─────    ─────
   6850    16928    11895     7895     8654
```

Addition 2-Digit Numbers

Day:  Time: Score: /30

1). 72
    +10
    ___

2). 45
    +41
    ___

3). 83
    +34
    ___

4). 55
    +41
    ___

5). 54
    +42
    ___

6). 41
    +49
    ___

7). 36
    +53
    ___

8). 81
    +65
    ___

9). 71
    +18
    ___

10). 24
    +51
    ___

11). 53
    +72
    ___

12). 12
    +48
    ___

13). 93
    +92
    ___

14). 26
    +56
    ___

15). 77
    +90
    ___

16). 53
    +23
    ___

17). 25
    +38
    ___

18). 81
    +15
    ___

19). 99
    +23
    ___

20). 13
    +31
    ___

21). 30
    +68
    ___

22). 66
    +29
    ___

23). 48
    +89
    ___

24). 83
    +15
    ___

25). 70
    +50
    ___

26). 38
    +37
    ___

27). 55
    +31
    ___

28). 43
    +28
    ___

29). 58
    +16
    ___

30). 90
    +88
    ___

1

Addition 2-Digit Numbers

Day:　　　Time:　　　Score:　　/30

1).　56　　2).　51　　3).　31　　4).　80　　5).　　9
　　+59　　　　+85　　　　+50　　　　+74　　　　+70

6).　　　　7).　　　　8).　　　　9).　　　　10).
　　74　　　　94　　　　45　　　　31　　　　68
　+37　　　+88　　　+19　　　+20　　　+75

11).　　　12).　　　13).　　　14).　　　15).
　　67　　　　28　　　　97　　　　88　　　　59
　+73　　　+47　　　+35　　　+63　　　　+9

16).　　　17).　　　18).　　　19).　　　20).
　　52　　　　54　　　　94　　　　12　　　　40
　+18　　　+33　　　+60　　　+76　　　+49

21).　　　22).　　　23).　　　24).　　　25).
　　58　　　　14　　　　72　　　　34　　　　33
　+83　　　　+9　　　+73　　　+93　　　+42

26).　　　27).　　　28).　　　29).　　　30).
　　87　　　　41　　　　25　　　　71　　　　78
　+91　　　+33　　　+93　　　+26　　　+94

2

Addition 2-Digit Numbers

Day:  Time: Score: /30

1). 28
   +41

2). 58
   +85

3). 14
   +27

4). 79
   +84

5). 81
   +24

6). 49
   +90

7). 76
   +81

8). 17
   +12

9). 42
   +78

10). 61
   +61

11). 75
   +97

12). 84
   +67

13). 49
   +98

14). 60
   +67

15). 68
   +15

16). 97
   +38

17). 58
   +33

18). 44
   +70

19). 55
   +85

20). 41
   +83

21). 10
   +70

22). 89
   +91

23). 45
   +29

24). 22
   +68

25). 97
   +71

26). 34
   +32

27). 19
   +67

28). 27
   +35

29). 94
   +86

30). 65
   +99

3

Addition 2-Digit Numbers

Day:  Time: Score: /30

1). 84 +51

2). 63 +53

3). 33 +82

4). 78 +65

5). 33 +68

6). 16 +34

7). 33 +94

8). 30 +91

9). 98 +90

10). 29 +76

11). 17 +30

12). 43 +35

13). 67 +63

14). 14 +52

15). 81 +32

16). 10 +44

17). 91 +81

18). 48 +98

19). 26 +52

20). 76 +35

21). 23 +93

22). 61 +46

23). 80 +49

24). 52 +86

25). 76 +9

26). 54 +21

27). 51 +72

28). 60 +97

29). 86 +49

30). 62 +87

4

Addition 3-Digit Numbers

Day:  Time: Score: /30

1). 546
    +817
    ____

2). 436
    +159
    ____

3). 482
    +120
    ____

4). 480
    +537
    ____

5). 366
    +321
    ____

6). 317
    +721
    ____

7). 116
    +918
    ____

8). 353
    +296
    ____

9). 707
    +160
    ____

10). 498
    +305
    ____

11). 485
    +837
    ____

12). 794
    +559
    ____

13). 443
    +245
    ____

14). 283
    +532
    ____

15). 382
    +297
    ____

16). 486
    +184
    ____

17). 513
    +524
    ____

18). 236
    +823
    ____

19). 810
    +598
    ____

20). 679
    +702
    ____

21). 611
    +495
    ____

22). 789
    +496
    ____

23). 398
    +402
    ____

24). 383
    +124
    ____

25). 816
    +474
    ____

26). 876
    +109
    ____

27). 668
    +638
    ____

28). 151
    +121
    ____

29). 529
    +933
    ____

30). 712
    +662
    ____

Addition 3-Digit Numbers

Day:  Time: Score: /30

1). 400
+749

2). 597
+327

3). 991
+752

4). 983
+254

5). 581
+357

6). 738
+854

7). 978
+115

8). 148
+172

9). 218
+808

10). 807
+352

11). 137
+110

12). 782
+607

13). 965
+920

14). 412
+513

15). 557
+676

16). 706
+836

17). 723
+668

18). 686
+741

19). 980
+410

20). 923
+222

21). 291
+154

22). 422
+423

23). 350
+402

24). 577
+916

25). 585
+275

26). 477
+344

27). 794
+271

28). 295
+662

29). 113
+101

30). 542
+986

Addition 3-Digit Numbers

Day:  Time: Score: /30

1). 149 +914

2). 178 +744

3). 370 +559

4). 307 +583

5). 846 +239

6). 204 +911

7). 556 +434

8). 242 +370

9). 226 +239

10). 718 +996

11). 930 +626

12). 869 +629

13). 624 +578

14). 463 +243

15). 191 +637

16). 351 +855

17). 283 +221

18). 732 +256

19). 945 +953

20). 273 +842

21). 643 +998

22). 285 +792

23). 917 +325

24). 566 +418

25). 820 +665

26). 289 +330

27). 617 +869

28). 212 +703

29). 955 +905

30). 973 +809

7

Addition 4-Digit Numbers

Day:  Time: Score: /30

1). 6660
   +3322

2). 7117
   +1037

3). 1650
   +9703

4). 6980
   +7291

5). 8447
   +5927

6). 9559
   +4973

7). 9189
   +2414

8). 2853
   +2672

9). 2665
   +7814

10). 8013
   +9971

11). 1406
   +7404

12). 2665
   +9919

13). 2568
   +1420

14). 9302
   +4253

15). 5952
   +9356

16). 7527
   +8047

17). 6250
   +1805

18). 9716
   +2659

19). 1802
   +4516

20). 2319
   +4065

21). 6477
   +4945

22). 1444
   +9951

23). 4997
   +2745

24). 5515
   +3199

25). 6958
   +8302

26). 3796
   +7736

27). 3064
   +5658

28). 4325
   +9076

29). 4569
   +2871

30). 7305
   +5251

10

Addition 4-Digit Numbers

Day:　　　　　Time:　　　　Score:　　/30

1). 2105
   +8861

2). 4961
   +4395

3). 3406
   +3214

4). 9089
   +1954

5). 6332
   +2194

6). 5876
   +1083

7). 2611
   +8116

8). 2456
   +6656

9). 2932
   +2109

10). 3025
   +5705

11). 6315
   +2254

12). 5193
   +6605

13). 9903
   +2796

14). 7987
   +6431

15). 4895
   +3752

16). 8570
   +3546

17). 8195
   +1695

18). 7947
   +3971

19). 2095
   +5235

20). 1619
   +4344

21). 6237
   +7712

22). 6396
   +9299

23). 9928
   +6949

24). 9362
   +4902

25). 2828
   +4461

26). 3277
   +2396

27). 3971
   +2392

28). 4549
   +4869

29). 9037
   +3585

30). 8271
   +5608

11

Addition 4-Digit Numbers

Day:  **Time:** **Score:** **/30**

1). 7465
+6793

2). 2497
+6615

3). 5926
+5030

4). 8196
+9719

5). 3743
+2510

6). 9819
+8797

7). 6226
+9616

8). 7283
+5732

9). 3171
+7887

10). 6001
+8135

11). 1613
+1168

12). 1652
+3018

13). 2169
+7076

14). 4705
+6001

15). 1853
+5715

16). 8117
+9051

17). 6722
+6915

18). 5993
+4638

19). 8179
+1926

20). 8829
+2851

21). 7254
+7421

22). 3383
+7444

23). 2754
+5846

24). 8142
+7017

25). 3708
+1666

26). 4817
+6523

27). 8172
+9813

28). 4277
+8094

29). 4066
+1674

30). 4882
+8712

Subtraction

12 worksheets
30 problems per sheet

William. Education

Examples

Example 1 (2-digit numbers)

①
```
  95
- 46
----
```

②
```
   8 15
   9̷5̷
     ↓
-  46
----
    9
```

③
```
   8 15
   9̷5̷
     ↓
-  46
----
   49
```

Example 2 (3-digit numbers)

①
```
  813
-  75
----
```

②
```
   0 13
  81̷3̷
     ↓
-   75
----
     8
```

③
```
  7 10 13
  8̷1̷3̷
     ↓
-   75
----
   38
```

④
```
  7 10 13
  8̷1̷3̷
    ↓
-   75
----
  738
```

Example 3 (3-digit numbers)

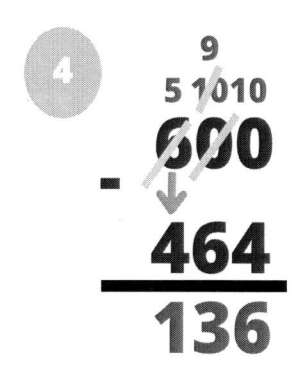

①
```
  600
- 464
----
```

②
```
      9
   5 1̷0 10
   6̷0̷0̷
     ↓
-  464
----
     6
```

③
```
      9
   5 1̷0 10
   6̷0̷0̷
     ↓
-  464
----
    36
```

④
```
      9
   5 1̷0 10
   6̷0̷0̷
     ↓
-  464
----
   136
```

Example 4 (2-digit numbers)

⁸15	⁷14		³10	
- 9̶5̶	- 8̶4̶	- 87	- 4̶0̶	- 56
66	18	70	22	26
29	66	17	18	30

	⁴16			
- 88	- 5̶6̶	- 29	- 99	- 59
28	18	20	44	51
60	38	9	55	8

Example 5 (3-digit numbers)

⁴10	¹11	⁵14	⁶11	⁹ ⁷10 15
- 3̶5̶0	- 2̶1̶6	- 2̶6̶4	- 7̶1̶9	- 8̶0̶5̶
236	193	229	64	67
114	23	35	655	738

⁸ ¹² 2̶ 10	⁴12	⁴13	⁴10	¹³ 4 3̶ 14
- 9̶3̶0̶	- 7̶5̶2	- 9̶5̶3	- 6̶5̶0	- 5̶4̶4̶
786	126	138	44	58
144	626	815	606	486

Example 6 (4-digit numbers)

³10			⁴13	¹³ 3̶ 3 14
- 1̶4̶04	- 3578	- 5678	- 37̶5̶3	- 4̶4̶4̶9̶
1080	1563	2528	244	855
324	2015	3150	3509	3594

⁸11	¹14	⁴10	⁶13 5 10	11 16 7̶ 1̶ 6 10
- 1̶9̶19	- 1̶2̶43	- 5̶0̶55	- 7̶3̶6̶0̶	- 8̶2̶7̶0̶
1632	1191	1211	535	384
287	52	3844	6825	7886

Subtraction 2-Digit Numbers

Day:  Time: Score: /30

1). 76
    -29

2). 78
    -61

3). 25
    -24

4). 12
    -9

5). 28
    -18

6). 76
    -62

7). 97
    -79

8). 71
    -59

9). 40
    -23

10). 50
    -31

11). 74
    -45

12). 94
    -59

13). 68
    -9

14). 23
    -11

15). 36
    -23

16). 39
    -18

17). 49
    -18

18). 93
    -46

19). 42
    -11

20). 33
    -30

21). 97
    -61

22). 37
    -35

23). 10
    -9

24). 14
    -13

25). 36
    -23

26). 22
    -9

27). 95
    -54

28). 18
    -15

29). 93
    -38

30). 91
    -58

13

Subtraction 2-Digit Numbers

Day:　　　　　Time:　　　　　Score: /30

1) 72
   -57

2) 28
   -15

3) 41
   -40

4) 19
   -14

5) 60
   -44

6) 80
   -64

7) 31
   -30

8) 37
   -32

9) 99
   -91

10) 48
    -16

11) 93
    -18

12) 45
    -13

13) 78
    -19

14) 45
    -13

15) 71
    -35

16) 16
    -11

17) 23
    -17

18) 41
    -29

19) 61
    -18

20) 31
    -24

21) 63
    -58

22) 74
    -44

23) 49
    -36

24) 76
    -14

25) 89
    -69

26) 37
    -26

27) 72
    -66

28) 43
    -17

29) 48
    -29

30) 40
    -21

Subtraction 2-Digit Numbers

Day:  Time: Score: /30

1). 68
   -31

2). 17
   -11

3). 55
   -41

4). 66
   -33

5). 53
   -43

6). 51
   -9

7). 72
   -24

8). 69
   -39

9). 87
   -81

10). 26
    -21

11). 10
    -10

12). 74
    -72

13). 19
    -17

14). 62
    -47

15). 60
    -26

16). 55
    -29

17). 67
    -23

18). 15
    -13

19). 22
    -12

20). 85
    -24

21). 69
    -66

22). 91
    -27

23). 23
    -22

24). 37
    -19

25). 50
    -43

26). 64
    -31

27). 12
    -9

28). 35
    -21

29). 32
    -24

30). 72
    -57

Subtraction 2-Digit Numbers

Day:  Time: Score: /30

1). 74
   -14

2). 45
   -24

3). 12
   -11

4). 84
   -18

5). 97
   -69

6). 36
   -10

7). 31
   -11

8). 44
   -39

9). 59
   -55

10). 50
    -25

11). 18
    -13

12). 18
    -17

13). 99
    -90

14). 80
    -12

15). 21
    -9

16). 36
    -13

17). 62
    -22

18). 22
    -13

19). 45
    -34

20). 21
    -10

21). 27
    -26

22). 87
    -11

23). 88
    -77

24). 30
    -12

25). 44
    -19

26). 19
    -16

27). 38
    -33

28). 52
    -10

29). 92
    -30

30). 97
    -45

16

Subtraction 3-Digit Numbers

Day:  **Time:** **Score:** /30

1). 584
    -554

2). 436
    -310

3). 543
    -122

4). 443
    -204

5). 380
    -234

6). 249
    -146

7). 917
    -268

8). 207
    -128

9). 710
    -513

10). 739
    -234

11). 723
    -639

12). 338
    -177

13). 895
    -332

14). 529
    -429

15). 525
    -371

16). 856
    -554

17). 633
    -295

18). 693
    -685

19). 595
    -388

20). 127
    -110

21). 435
    -169

22). 275
    -107

23). 435
    -251

24). 977
    -320

25). 314
    -203

26). 610
    -144

27). 790
    -154

28). 857
    -213

29). 761
    -172

30). 488
    -454

Subtraction 3-Digit Numbers

Day:  **Time:** **Score:** /30

1). 403 −245

2). 394 −117

3). 962 −661

4). 718 −671

5). 174 −133

6). 674 −116

7). 988 −733

8). 346 −273

9). 553 −175

10). 749 −367

11). 615 −431

12). 744 −463

13). 738 −608

14). 602 −377

15). 650 −645

16). 713 −307

17). 152 −129

18). 105 −100

19). 574 −105

20). 130 −123

21). 483 −202

22). 229 −126

23). 723 −484

24). 898 −266

25). 567 −346

26). 238 −110

27). 464 −126

28). 975 −280

29). 366 −213

30). 421 −402

Subtraction 3-Digit Numbers

Day:  **Time:** **Score:** /30

1). 631 −592

2). 948 −259

3). 791 −164

4). 845 −353

5). 875 −380

6). 270 −181

7). 982 −407

8). 103 −100

9). 224 −199

10). 246 −116

11). 648 −248

12). 556 −529

13). 657 −388

14). 865 −793

15). 560 −342

16). 690 −116

17). 843 −812

18). 970 −841

19). 634 −599

20). 272 −247

21). 535 −277

22). 410 −185

23). 434 −162

24). 438 −358

25). 364 −232

26). 370 −194

27). 774 −360

28). 944 −424

29). 803 −506

30). 303 −237

19

Subtraction 3-Digit Numbers

Day:  Time: Score: /30

1). 851 -598

2). 714 -110

3). 727 -402

4). 861 -409

5). 163 -150

6). 951 -534

7). 415 -177

8). 442 -179

9). 571 -218

10). 213 -157

11). 784 -522

12). 524 -327

13). 687 -510

14). 486 -216

15). 928 -716

16). 305 -168

17). 795 -319

18). 267 -137

19). 781 -517

20). 911 -791

21). 878 -757

22). 234 -223

23). 845 -721

24). 176 -161

25). 162 -123

26). 430 -270

27). 564 -110

28). 611 -107

29). 567 -205

30). 867 -858

Subtraction 4-Digit Numbers

Day:  Time: Score: /30

1). 6458
   -3004

2). 9535
   -3079

3). 7493
   -3607

4). 5721
   -4225

5). 2515
   -2422

6). 8555
   -4019

7). 8280
   -5084

8). 4270
   -2177

9). 9806
   -1179

10). 2696
    -2178

11). 8321
    -6906

12). 6913
    -6454

13). 9376
    -8494

14). 3255
    -2497

15). 3966
    -1777

16). 5210
    -3332

17). 7022
    -6466

18). 9683
    -1874

19). 2225
    -1318

20). 1543
    -1431

21). 9688
    -1623

22). 8390
    -7251

23). 3686
    -1293

24). 3975
    -2691

25). 5279
    -1940

26). 4791
    -3078

27). 1380
    -1241

28). 1909
    -1401

29). 7518
    -5642

30). 2281
    -1581

21

Subtraction 4-Digit Numbers

Day: Time: Score: /30

1). 5850
   -2451

2). 9484
   -7525

3). 8157
   -7565

4). 1093
   -1021

5). 7237
   -2777

6). 1805
   -1162

7). 2296
   -1368

8). 3304
   -2276

9). 5149
   -3426

10). 4432
    -3871

11). 3772
    -2988

12). 5604
    -5281

13). 7824
    -5474

14). 4508
    -3266

15). 7006
    -1154

16). 3385
    -1373

17). 3949
    -1682

18). 8050
    -6544

19). 2443
    -1361

20). 9439
    -2613

21). 1205
    -1119

22). 7860
    -2328

23). 6061
    -5270

24). 7333
    -4633

25). 9359
    -7831

26). 4358
    -4117

27). 1684
    -1219

28). 7218
    -2938

29). 8449
    -2064

30). 3427
    -2801

Subtraction 4-Digit Numbers

Day:  **Time:** **Score:** /30

1). 5076 −4508
2). 7560 −6001
3). 8047 −5001
4). 4840 −2107
5). 5601 −2990

6). 8928 −7378
7). 9992 −5823
8). 1025 −1023
9). 6412 −4154
10). 8195 −6227

11). 4552 −1546
12). 9797 −8161
13). 3623 −1860
14). 2945 −1746
15). 9031 −2444

16). 1685 −1027
17). 3643 −2811
18). 7823 −2560
19). 9477 −8380
20). 7275 −6712

21). 5922 −3970
22). 3547 −2881
23). 1088 −1026
24). 8542 −3539
25). 3708 −3615

26). 4135 −2441
27). 3052 −1754
28). 4101 −3322
29). 1733 −1689
30). 7836 −4513

Subtraction 4-Digit Numbers

Day:  Time: Score: /30

1). 6753
   -5686

2). 4954
   -4647

3). 7092
   -2725

4). 6261
   -4114

5). 3166
   -1702

6). 8074
   -2656

7). 6442
   -5565

8). 1274
   -1252

9). 2538
   -2460

10). 4180
    -4152

11). 9235
    -6906

12). 6986
    -5510

13). 3603
    -1167

14). 4227
    -3681

15). 9434
    -5266

16). 2654
    -1050

17). 8596
    -5487

18). 3625
    -2680

19). 4232
    -1234

20). 8128
    -4124

21). 8704
    -6251

22). 6876
    -3065

23). 7040
    -1235

24). 3458
    -2469

25). 4211
    -3239

26). 6416
    -3028

27). 2947
    -1967

28). 3258
    -2411

29). 5960
    -3182

30). 6817
    -2124

24

Multiplication ✖

12 worksheets
30 problems per sheet

William. Education

Examples

Example 1 (2-digit by 1-digit numbers)

①
   95
 × 5
 ———

②
   ²95
 × 5
 ———
    5

③
   ²95
 × 5
 ———
  475

Example 2 (3-digit by 1-digit numbers)

①
   346
 ×   8
 ————

②
   3⁴46
 ×   8
 ————
      8

③
   ³⁴46
 ×   8
 ————
     68

④
   ³⁴46
 ×   8
 ————
   2768

Example 3 (4-digit by 1-digit numbers)

①
   2435
 ×   6
 ————

②
   24³5
 ×   6
 ————
      0

③
   2²³35
 ×   6
 ————
     10

④
   ²²⁴35
 ×   6
 ————
    610

⑤
   ²²⁴35
 ×   6
 ————
  14610

Example 4 (5-digit by 1-digit numbers)

①
   42563
 ×   6
 ————

②
   4256¹3
 ×   6
 ————
       8

③
   425³6¹3
 ×   6
 ————
      78

④
   4²5³6¹3
 ×   6
 ————
     378

⑤+
   ¹4²5³6¹3
 ×   6
 ————
   255378

Example 5 (3-digit by 3-digit numbers)

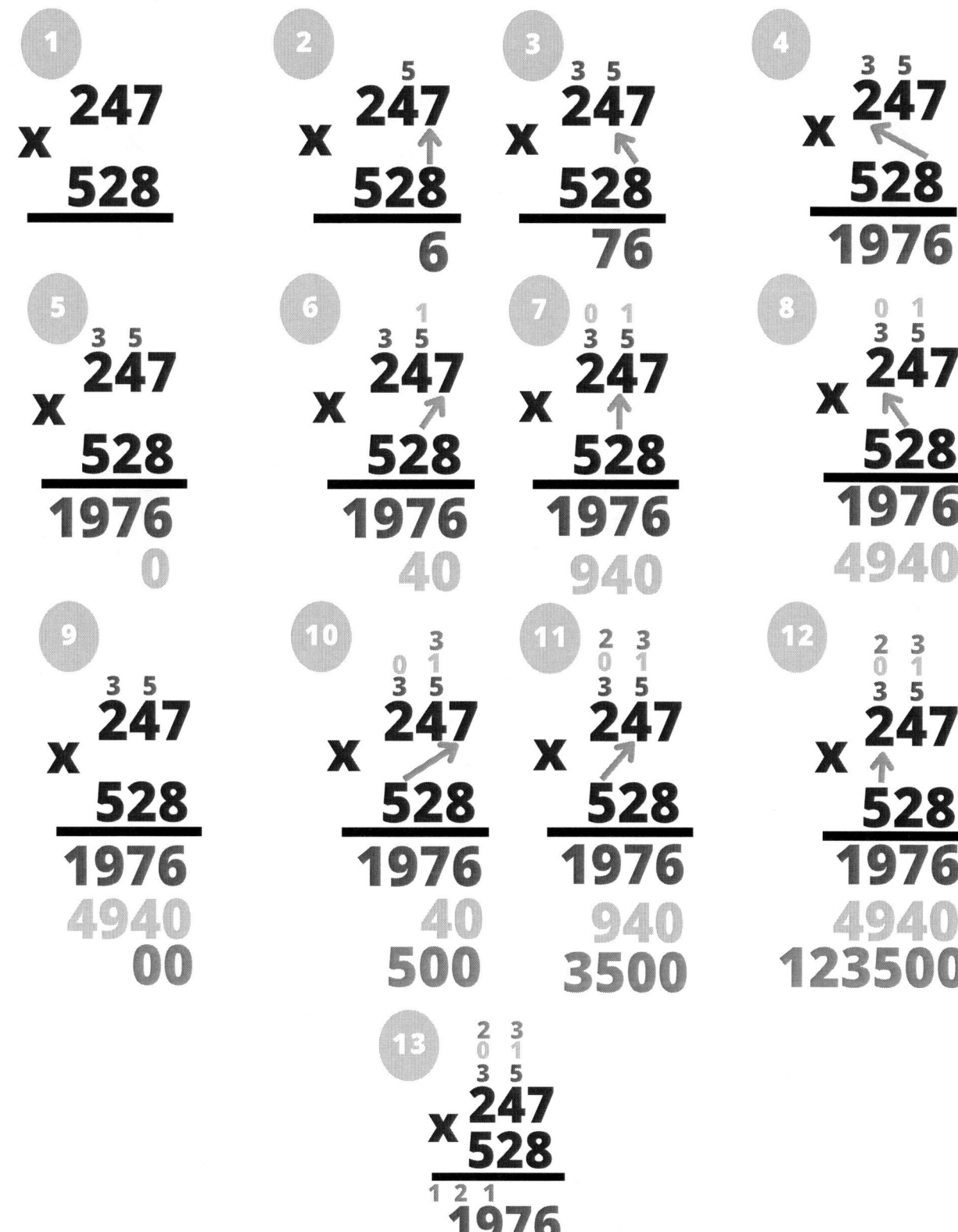

Example 6 (2-digit by 2-digit numbers)

1)
```
   45
×  95
─────
```

2)
```
   ²
   45
×  95
─────
    5
```

3)
```
   ²
   45
×  95
─────
  225
```

4)
```
   ²
   45
×  95
─────
  225
    0
```

5)
```
   ⁴
   ²
   45
×  95
─────
  225
   50
```

6)
```
   ⁴
   ²
   45
×  95
─────
  225
 4050
```

7)
```
     ⁴
     ²
     45
  ×  95
  ─────
    225
+  4050
  ─────
   4275
```

Multiplication 2-Digit By 1-Digit Numbers

Day: Time: Score: /30

1). 78   2). 17   3). 31   4). 46   5). 80
    x3   x3   x3   x4   x8

6).   7).   8).   9).   10).
    76   89   12   75   39
    x6   x7   x5   x3   x8

11).   12).   13).   14).   15).
    81   44   79   43   48
    x4   x4   x5   x7   x8

16).   17).   18).   19).   20).
    41   91   82   51   47
    x4   x9   x5   x6   x4

21).   22).   23).   24).   25).
    32   90   9   93   97
    x4   x7   x7   x9   x6

26).   27).   28).   29).   30).
    67   44   45   45   41
    x7   x7   x2   x3   x3

Multiplication 2-Digit By 1-Digit Numbers

Day: Time: Score: /30

1) 52   2) 47   3)   9   4) 58   5) 33
    x4   x9   x4   x4   x7

6) 11   7) 71   8) 37   9) 89   10) 91
    x4   x8   x7   x2   x5

11) 56   12) 63   13) 94   14) 28   15) 34
    x6   x2   x5   x4   x4

16) 26   17) 23   18) 66   19) 56   20) 37
    x3   x5   x4   x9   x9

21) 89   22) 61   23) 19   24) 90   25) 42
    x8   x5   x4   x8   x4

26) 22   27) 56   28) 11   29) 57   30) 10
    x4   x7   x6   x5   x4

Multiplication 2-Digit By 1-Digit Numbers

Day: **Time:**   **Score:**   /30

1). 32
×9

2). 10
×7

3). 31
×6

4). 71
×8

5). 60
×8

6). 65
×5

7). 97
×8

8). 43
×5

9). 85
×9

10). 52
×4

11). 87
×3

12). 84
×6

13). 30
×4

14). 66
×8

15). 14
×8

16). 23
×8

17). 64
×4

18). 65
×7

19). 63
×6

20). 13
×3

21). 61
×5

22). 64
×6

23). 99
×4

24). 49
×3

25). 23
×3

26). 63
×8

27). 73
×4

28). 15
×7

29). 16
×6

30). 42
×4

Multiplication 2-Digit By 1-Digit Numbers

Day: Time: Score: /30

1). 81 x4
2). 38 x6
3). 93 x8
4). 20 x8
5). 36 x9

6). 81 x5
7). 31 x8
8). 16 x8
9). 37 x6
10). 47 x8

11). 27 x7
12). 40 x6
13). 45 x4
14). 9 x4
15). 43 x8

16). 23 x4
17). 58 x5
18). 22 x3
19). 36 x9
20). 44 x6

21). 74 x3
22). 33 x3
23). 95 x7
24). 14 x4
25). 18 x3

26). 39 x9
27). 62 x2
28). 77 x3
29). 52 x6
30). 30 x6

Multiplication 2-Digit By 2-Digit Numbers

Day:　　　　　Time:　　　　　Score: /30

1). 48
    x70

2). 75
    x92

3). 28
    x57

4). 92
    x65

5). 39
    x53

6). 16
    x48

7). 53
    x45

8). 84
    x53

9). 70
    x39

10). 55
     x40

11). 35
     x14

12). 46
     x94

13). 22
     x43

14). 50
     x53

15). 28
     x92

16). 43
     x20

17). 93
     x60

18). 81
     x12

19). 83
     x86

20). 37
     x39

21). 10
     x68

22). 31
     x81

23). 20
     x27

24). 10
     x46

25). 52
     x91

26). 58
     x12

27). 80
     x26

28). 33
     x30

29). 37
     x83

30). 28
     x84

Multiplication 2-Digit By 2-Digit Numbers

Day: Time: Score: /30

1). 88   2). 16   3). 58   4). 96   5). 72
    x97   x92   x92   x91   x39

6). 76   7). 56   8). 74   9). 30   10). 68
    x64   x89   x32   x17   x48

11). 10   12). 46   13). 91   14). 24   15). 19
    x14   x89   x79   x62   x97

16). 49   17). 16   18). 77   19). 11   20). 38
    x92   x61   x42   x12   x73

21). 71   22). 30   23). 84   24). 60   25). 42
    x50   x42   x74   x38   x71

26). 49   27). 56   28). 96   29). 78   30). 80
    x58   x11   x84   x73   x60

Multiplication 2-Digit By 2-Digit Numbers

Day: **Time:**   **Score:** /30

1)   39
    x71

2)   79
    x39

3)   60
    x60

4)   11
    x59

5)   74
    x17

6)   74
    x18

7)   23
    x53

8)   49
    x49

9)   82
    x75

10)   44
    x94

11)   91
    x55

12)   15
    x22

13)   80
    x71

14)   65
    x51

15)   45
    x68

16)   14
    x50

17)   56
    x55

18)   68
    x18

19)   92
    x74

20)   45
    x89

21)   62
    x59

22)   88
    x70

23)   19
    x84

24)   55
    x36

25)   76
    x80

26)   78
    x81

27)   13
    x13

28)   21
    x83

29)   15
    x66

30)   27
    x62

Multiplication 2-Digit By 2-Digit Numbers

Day: Time: Score: /30

1). 72   2). 77   3). 65   4). 61   5). 86
    x72   x20   x53   x51   x37

6). 88   7). 75   8). 46   9). 37   10). 56
    x48   x68   x14   x66   x93

11). 60   12). 93   13). 62   14). 83   15). 90
     x26   x26   x52   x74   x56

16). 18   17). 39   18). 20   19). 61   20). 66
     x68   x69   x56   x27   x82

21). 35   22). 66   23). 75   24). 19   25). 71
     x23   x19   x30   x34   x26

26). 95   27). 68   28). 17   29). 71   30). 9
     x65   x40   x49   x52   x10

Multiplication 3-Digit By 3-Digit Numbers

Day: **Time:**   **Score:** /30

1). 178 x819

2). 587 x637

3). 439 x543

4). 883 x590

5). 934 x247

6). 804 x964

7). 322 x435

8). 935 x595

9). 303 x508

10). 375 x841

11). 985 x607

12). 566 x175

13). 431 x127

14). 169 x783

15). 924 x527

16). 705 x617

17). 986 x818

18). 802 x964

19). 243 x609

20). 604 x383

21). 953 x610

22). 590 x308

23). 354 x362

24). 298 x590

25). 355 x890

26). 334 x205

27). 393 x681

28). 835 x651

29). 503 x677

30). 960 x191

Multiplication 3-Digit By 3-Digit Numbers

Day: Time: Score: /30

1) 475
    x830

2) 796
    x334

3) 735
    x803

4) 400
    x905

5) 782
    x814

6) 306
    x768

7) 420
    x866

8) 962
    x601

9) 252
    x730

10) 673
    x708

11) 521
    x614

12) 838
    x808

13) 898
    x245

14) 740
    x973

15) 641
    x244

16) 554
    x275

17) 222
    x815

18) 775
    x632

19) 692
    x233

20) 993
    x455

21) 987
    x287

22) 654
    x660

23) 791
    x934

24) 812
    x303

25) 319
    x896

26) 678
    x710

27) 748
    x559

28) 348
    x714

29) 543
    x253

30) 201
    x981

Multiplication 3-Digit By 3-Digit Numbers

Day: **Time:** **Score:** /30

1). 913 x302

2). 682 x250

3). 670 x314

4). 737 x418

5). 470 x735

6). 148 x536

7). 562 x421

8). 256 x935

9). 902 x531

10). 346 x218

11). 510 x729

12). 593 x560

13). 492 x149

14). 962 x871

15). 125 x651

16). 841 x291

17). 266 x581

18). 293 x433

19). 272 x418

20). 227 x973

21). 443 x479

22). 358 x926

23). 244 x931

24). 222 x366

25). 391 x649

26). 198 x276

27). 555 x451

28). 579 x925

29). 522 x321

30). 151 x841

Multiplication 3-Digit By 3-Digit Numbers

Day:　　　　　Time:　　　　　Score:　　/30

1).　748　　2).　802　　3).　976　　4).　440　　5).　731
　　x632　　　　x259　　　　x346　　　　x444　　　　x465

6).　685　　7).　709　　8).　660　　9).　626　　10).　314
　　x290　　　　x174　　　　x760　　　　x330　　　　x872

11).　129　　12).　904　　13).　485　　14).　602　　15).　165
　　x309　　　　x612　　　　x506　　　　x827　　　　x748

16).　735　　17).　306　　18).　154　　19).　320　　20).　444
　　x751　　　　x616　　　　x534　　　　x295　　　　x277

21).　347　　22).　428　　23).　611　　24).　127　　25).　795
　　x649　　　　x637　　　　x643　　　　x953　　　　x702

26).　915　　27).　290　　28).　644　　29).　676　　30).　503
　　x442　　　　x735　　　　x314　　　　x633　　　　x344

Division ÷

15 worksheets
40 problems per sheet

William. Education

Examples

Quotient

Divisor ⌐ Dividend

Dividend ÷ Divisor = Quotient

Steps

D = Divide
M = Multiply
S = Subtract
B = Bring down

Example:

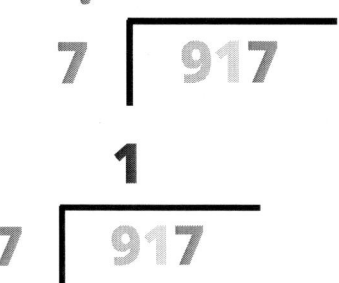

7 ⌐ 917

```
   1
7 ⌐ 917
```

Step 1: D for Divide

How many times will 7 go into 917? That's too hard to work out in your head, so let's break it down into smaller steps.
The first problem you'll work out in this equation is how many times can you divide 9 into 7. The answer is 1. So you put 1 on the quotient line.

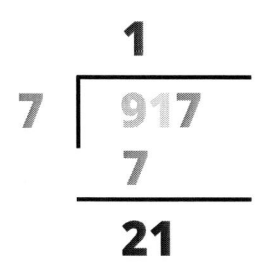

```
   1
7 ⌐ 917
     7
```

Step 2: M for Multiply

You multiply your answer from step 1 and your divisor: 1 x 7 = 7. You write 7 under the 9

```
   1
7 ⌐ 917
     7
   ___
     2
```

Step 3: S for Subtract

Next you subtract. In this case it will be 9 – 7 = 2

```
   1
7 ⌐ 917
     7
   ___
    21
```

Step 4: B for Bring down

The last step in the sequence is to bring down the next number from the dividend, which in this case is 1. You write the 1 next to the 2, making the number 21.

Now you start all over again

```
   13
7 ⌐ 917
     7
   ___
    21
```

Step 1: D for Divide

How many times can you divide 3 into 21. The answer is 3. So you put 3 on the quotient line.

```
   13
7 ⌐ 917
     7
   ___
    21
    21
```

Step 2: M for Multiply

You multiply your answer from step 1 and your divisor: 3 x 7 = 21. You write 21 under the 21

Step 1: D for Divide

How many times can you divide 7 into 7. The answer is 1. So you put 1 on the quotient line.

```
    131
 7 )917
    7
    21
    21
    07
```

Step 2: M for Multiply

You multiply your answer from step 1 and your divisor: 1 × 7 = 7. You write 7 under the 7

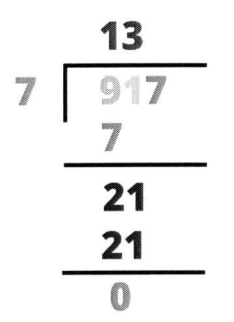

Step 3: S for Subtract

Next you subtract. In this case it will be 21 − 21 = 0

Step 4: B for Bring down

The last step in the sequence is to bring down the next number from the dividend, which in this case is 7. You write the 7 next to the 0, making the number 7.

Now you start all over again

Step 1: D for Divide (repeat)

```
    131
 7 )917
    7
    21
    21
    07
     7
```

Step 3: S for Subtract

Next you subtract. In this case it will be 7 − 7 = 0

```
    131
 7 )917
    7
    21
    21
    07
     7
     0
```

There is no need for step 4. We have finished the problem.

Once you have the answer, do the problem in reverse using multiplication (7 × 131 = 917) to make sure your answer is correct.

Division 5-digit by 2

```
        00309
    88 )27218
      -    0
          27
      -    0
         272
      - 264
          81
      -    0
         818
      - 792
          26
```

27218 divided by 88 equals 309 with a remainder of 26

Division 3-digit by 2

```
          007
    45 )323
      -   0
         32
      -   0
        323
      -315
          8
```

323 divided by 45 equals 7 with a remainder of 8

Division 4-digit by 1

```
         0928
     8 )7426
      -   0
         74
      - 72
          22
      - 16
          66
      - 64
           2
```

7426 divided by 8 equals 928 with a remainder of 2

Division 4-digit by 2

```
         0132
    32 )4236
      -   0
         42
      - 32
        103
      - 96
         76
      - 64
         12
```

4236 divided by 32 equals 132 with a remainder of 12

Division 5-digit by 1

```
      03685
   ┌────────
 9 │ 33169
   -  0
   ───
      33
   -  27
      ───
       61
   -   54
       ───
        76
   -    72
        ───
         49
   -     45
         ───
          4
```

33169 divided by 9 equals 3685 with a remainder of 4

Once you have the answer, do the problem in reverse using multiplication (9 x 3685+4 = 33169) to make sure your answer is correct.

Division 3-digit by 1

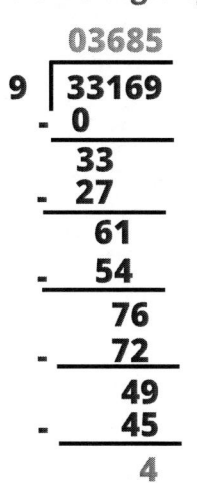

```
      092
   ┌──────
 7 │ 648
   -  0
   ───
      64
   -  63
      ───
       18
   -   14
       ───
        4
```

648 divided by 7 equals 92 with a remainder of 4

Once you have the answer, do the problem in reverse using multiplication (7 x 92+4 = 648) to make sure your answer is correct.

Division 4-digit by 1

```
      0553
   ┌───────
 5 │ 2767
   -  0
   ───
      27
   -  25
      ───
       26
   -   25
       ───
        17
   -    15
        ───
         2
```

2767 divided by 5 equals 553 with a remainder of 2

Once you have the answer, do the problem in reverse using multiplication (5 x 553+2 = 2767) to make sure your answer is correct.

Division 6-digit by 1

```
      065282
   ┌─────────
 7 │ 456978
   -  0
   ───
      45
   -  42
      ───
       36
   -   35
       ───
        19
   -    14
        ───
         57
   -     56
         ───
          18
   -      14
          ───
           4
```

456978 divided by 7 equals 65282 with a remainder of 4

Once you have the answer, do the problem in reverse using multiplication (7 x 65282+4 = 456978) to make sure your answer is correct.

Division 5-digit by 2

```
       02883
    ┌────────
 12 │ 34598
    -  0
    ───
       34
    -  24
       ───
       105
    -   96
       ───
        99
    -   96
        ───
         38
    -    36
         ───
          2
```

34598 divided by 12 equals 2883 with a remainder of 2

Once you have the answer, do the problem in reverse using multiplication (12 x 2883+2 = 34598) to make sure your answer is correct.

Division 3-digit by 2

```
       006
    ┌──────
 89 │ 536
    -  0
    ───
       53
    -   0
       ───
       536
    -  534
       ───
         2
```

536 divided by 89 equals 6 with a remainder of 2

Once you have the answer, do the problem in reverse using multiplication (89 x 6+2 = 536) to make sure your answer is correct.

Division 4-digit by 1

```
      0949
   ┌───────
 6 │ 5698
   -  0
   ───
      56
   -  54
      ───
       29
   -   24
       ───
        58
   -    54
        ───
         4
```

5698 divided by 6 equals 949 with a remainder of 4

Once you have the answer, do the problem in reverse using multiplication (949 x 6+4 = 5698) to make sure your answer is correct.

Division 4-digit by 2

```
       0179
    ┌───────
 19 │ 3417
    -  0
    ───
       34
    -  19
       ───
       151
    -  133
       ───
       187
    -  171
       ───
        16
```

3417 divided by 19 equals 179 with a remainder of 16

Once you have the answer, do the problem in reverse using multiplication (179 x 19+16 = 3417) to make sure your answer is correct.

⚠ **Once you have the answer, do the problem in reverse using multiplication (Quotient x Divisor+Remainder = Dividend) to make sure your answer is correct.**

Division 2-Digit By 1-Digit Numbers

Day: Time: Score: /40

3⟌19   7⟌67   3⟌36   8⟌17   6⟌63

5⟌77   7⟌36   4⟌97   5⟌57   4⟌70

4⟌79   7⟌61   4⟌86   7⟌84   2⟌30

3⟌49   8⟌57   7⟌43   4⟌32   5⟌58

9⟌37   5⟌85   5⟌77   7⟌60   6⟌13

8⟌34   8⟌82   7⟌38   4⟌32   7⟌81

7⟌47   2⟌73   5⟌88   4⟌98   4⟌25

9⟌101   5⟌80   7⟌64   6⟌18   5⟌85

Division 2-Digit By 1-Digit Numbers

Day:　　　　Time:　　　　Score:　　/40

6)84　　2)96　　7)79　　5)83　　4)63

7)84　　3)38　　2)66　　7)70　　5)21

4)49　　4)14　　9)40　　5)88　　7)66

3)72　　6)26　　3)23　　6)36　　4)54

5)55　　6)40　　7)49　　5)72　　6)71

9)87　　3)61　　3)76　　4)22　　3)65

4)15　　2)16　　8)78　　2)71　　7)48

2)45　　9)68　　5)62　　8)67　　4)54

Division 2-Digit By 1-Digit Numbers

Day:　　　　Time:　　　　Score:　　　/40

4 | 50　　3 | 80　　5 | 76　　8 | 29　　4 | 81

3 | 92　　7 | 94　　6 | 70　　5 | 77　　5 | 53

2 | 43　　3 | 57　　8 | 52　　5 | 19　　4 | 21

3 | 10　　9 | 13　　6 | 90　　8 | 30　　6 | 83

5 | 76　　2 | 68　　8 | 18　　8 | 102　　6 | 81

6 | 54　　7 | 15　　7 | 30　　6 | 12　　8 | 64

6 | 31　　4 | 77　　5 | 12　　4 | 39　　4 | 23

7 | 96　　4 | 22　　8 | 86　　2 | 76　　4 | 42

Division 2-Digit By 1-Digit Numbers

Day: Time: Score: /40

7)89   2)31   2)79   7)12   6)61

7)56   3)40   7)31   2)93   6)82

7)44   3)59   8)81   3)73   2)22

7)56   5)52   7)98   8)60   7)51

3)30   8)20   8)14   4)27   8)101

3)66   6)79   4)61   3)96   3)28

9)87   7)39   7)86   3)63   6)21

6)88   4)89   8)75   6)41   9)22

Division 3-Digit By 1-Digit Numbers

Day: Time: Score: /40

5) 288   4) 362   3) 769   8) 883   3) 621

8) 151   3) 355   4) 339   4) 138   8) 909

3) 733   6) 696   4) 847   7) 738   3) 395

7) 471   7) 441   6) 490   5) 611   8) 266

2) 101   3) 868   4) 532   3) 171   7) 752

7) 592   6) 956   6) 922   2) 468   6) 819

4) 181   7) 212   8) 622   8) 323   6) 229

4) 751   5) 837   2) 426   2) 140   5) 646

Division 3-Digit By 1-Digit Numbers

Day: **Time:**   **Score:**   **/40**

9) 491   8) 346   6) 523   6) 973   4) 509

5) 211   6) 172   9) 457   4) 729   6) 274

2) 456   4) 964   7) 981   6) 177   8) 929

6) 680   4) 146   5) 754   5) 711   5) 642

5) 407   9) 240   5) 226   7) 307   3) 935

8) 674   4) 973   4) 449   3) 949   4) 398

8) 244   3) 698   8) 976   4) 657   7) 115

7) 835   4) 217   4) 346   5) 957   8) 398

42

Division 3-Digit By 1-Digit Numbers

Day: **Time:**   **Score:**   /40

2) 896   8) 683   2) 398   2) 855   7) 961

7) 650   7) 346   2) 766   4) 349   5) 321

4) 542   8) 197   8) 177   8) 193   7) 468

3) 188   4) 260   2) 693   7) 320   6) 578

6) 938   9) 983   8) 717   5) 297   7) 218

4) 552   5) 151   9) 669   9) 303   6) 201

4) 791   3) 799   2) 542   2) 530   9) 940

8) 356   3) 295   8) 445   5) 479   2) 264

Division 3-Digit By 1-Digit Numbers

Day: **Time:**   **Score:**   /40

6)243	4)141	3)840	2)796	8)247
8)685	5)147	8)219	3)148	3)539
8)150	8)212	5)777	7)130	3)301
5)624	3)251	8)252	7)730	5)296
8)529	3)796	7)763	6)585	8)619
6)559	8)962	8)118	7)812	4)662
4)368	2)160	6)642	7)318	4)661
7)351	6)247	5)539	6)375	4)659

Division 3-Digit By 2-Digit Numbers

Day:　　　　　Time:　　　　　Score:　　　／40

29)295　　89)323　　46)213　　38)619　　44)703

85)103　　55)618　　41)411　　91)638　　27)249

63)857　　66)541　　88)393　　36)817　　73)513

24)160　　19)804　　18)293　　13)180　　16)642

93)174　　51)183　　85)831　　62)981　　64)766

15)523　　37)763　　69)399　　31)1016　　70)991

72)468　　10)456　　28)926　　54)279　　97)766

48)835　　19)885　　57)64　　40)541　　21)129

Division 3-Digit By 2-Digit Numbers

Day: **Time:** **Score:** /40

29)810	26)218	96)99	56)576	55)776
33)621	99)212	95)557	26)248	89)675
59)722	31)242	32)243	16)429	39)818
54)1018	25)265	9)738	87)549	89)685
86)243	43)887	23)570	54)593	81)415
32)209	67)708	54)145	96)368	24)534
17)852	30)483	99)216	36)427	61)148
74)931	24)604	84)753	52)535	83)637

Division 3-Digit By 2-Digit Numbers

Day: Time: Score: /40

41)441   92)699   69)694   12)973   51)734

82)677   60)215   73)435   39)419   66)1042

96)473   32)889   49)155   26)459   26)903

72)143   72)649   55)162   31)656   33)344

38)377   46)485   57)869   63)244   89)208

97)286   84)694   89)638   29)739   19)679

57)825   17)480   69)597   83)650   89)521

38)937   72)329   99)864   10)695   75)397

Division 3-Digit By 2-Digit Numbers

Day: **Time:**   **Score:**   /40

44)697	58)126	33)537	31)743	65)809
63)897	18)549	93)604	51)226	94)673
85)826	35)742	70)105	69)316	60)380
23)473	35)112	14)436	80)488	60)547
71)231	44)419	11)869	38)942	70)214
18)162	12)753	31)173	52)726	29)221
63)312	37)219	26)804	64)897	47)281
43)243	95)539	85)694	95)973	81)428

48

Division 4-Digit By 2-Digit Numbers

Day: **Time:**   **Score:**   /40

30) 7768   51) 1234   70) 2417   45) 4954   9) 5222

61) 7723   56) 5143   67) 7846   81) 5870   70) 7624

14) 5787   9) 7582   97) 2534   83) 1073   71) 8626

54) 1446   49) 5853   82) 5039   11) 3324   23) 2957

49) 7678   42) 9789   62) 9490   67) 9508   18) 7000

96) 5478   57) 9816   58) 6734   65) 6215   76) 4466

91) 9796   10) 7269   50) 2714   84) 4489   50) 9747

41) 3259   64) 5445   41) 2779   55) 3634   60) 4722

Division 4-Digit By 2-Digit Numbers

Day: ⏱ **Time:**   **Score:**   **/40**

38)8434   44)3286   50)5535   29)8451   72)1386

67)9559   76)3587   90)4884   94)3182   48)7970

29)5887   44)5115   87)6519   23)9307   22)2377

65)2957   66)8750   79)9301   66)8385   92)5599

19)3442   70)4535   29)2764   50)4714   11)2299

48)3424   29)9126   27)1130   80)8840   11)8130

42)5395   25)2706   61)1099   56)6540   58)2212

78)3188   26)7161   11)1805   79)8728   16)2595

Division 4-Digit By 2-Digit Numbers

Day: **Time:**   **Score:**   /40

75)9339   31)9163   40)5544   82)5843   39)2835

85)3732   31)3704   86)9542   78)4481   23)3259

76)1626   9)5185   91)7578   87)5630   77)8905

72)9586   86)1655   64)1645   56)5786   42)4378

27)1155   95)9464   11)2115   85)3779   62)8800

97)2121   45)6217   97)5117   76)7666   55)1508

22)3175   76)2164   40)5812   51)8716   28)4390

93)2573   21)9649   38)8232   85)9743   72)8411

Fractions $\frac{A}{B}$

12 worksheets
40 problems per sheet

William. Education

Examples

Example 1 (Addition Of Fractions)

$$\frac{7}{5} + \frac{2}{6} = \frac{7(6)}{5(6)} + \frac{2(5)}{6(5)} = \frac{42}{30} + \frac{10}{30} = \frac{52 \div(2)}{30 \div(2)} = \boxed{\frac{26}{15}}$$

LCM
5:10,15,20,25,30
6:12,18,24,30

$$\frac{5}{4} + \frac{9}{7} = \frac{5(7)}{4(7)} + \frac{9(4)}{7(4)} = \frac{35}{28} + \frac{36}{28} = \boxed{\frac{71}{28}}$$

LCM
4: 8,12,16,20,24,28
7:14,21,28

Example 2 (Subtraction Of Fractions)

$$\frac{6}{4} - \frac{2}{5} = \frac{6(5)}{4(5)} - \frac{2(4)}{5(4)} = \frac{30}{20} - \frac{8}{20} = \frac{22 \div(2)}{20 \div(2)} = \boxed{\frac{11}{10}}$$

LCM
5:10,15,20
4:8,12,16,20

$$\frac{9}{2} - \frac{5}{8} = \frac{9(8)}{2(8)} - \frac{5(2)}{8(2)} = \frac{72}{16} - \frac{10}{16} = \frac{62 \div(2)}{16 \div(2)} = \boxed{\frac{31}{8}}$$

LCM
2: 4, 6, 8, 10, 12, 14, 16
8: 16

Example 3 (Multiplication Of Fractions)

$$\frac{8}{7} \times \frac{9}{3} = \frac{8 \times 9}{7 \times 3} = \frac{72 \div(3)}{21 \div(3)} = \boxed{\frac{24}{7}}$$

$$\frac{9}{5} \times \frac{4}{8} = \frac{9 \times 4}{5 \times 8} = \frac{36 \div(4)}{40 \div(4)} = \boxed{\frac{9}{10}}$$

Example 4 (Division Of Fractions)

$$\frac{5}{14} \div \frac{21}{9} = \frac{5 \times 9}{14 \times 21} = \frac{45 \div(3)}{294 \div(3)} = \boxed{\frac{15}{98}}$$

$$\begin{array}{r} 14 \\ \times\ 21 \\ \hline 14 \\ +\ 28\ \ \\ \hline 294 \end{array}$$

$$\frac{9}{8} \div \frac{7}{5} = \frac{9 \times 5}{8 \times 7} = \boxed{\frac{45}{56}}$$

Adding Fractions

Day: Time: Score: /40

1) $\dfrac{3}{5} + \dfrac{1}{15} =$

2) $\dfrac{1}{6} + \dfrac{5}{6} =$

3) $\dfrac{6}{7} + \dfrac{4}{7} =$

4) $\dfrac{4}{7} + \dfrac{1}{3} =$

5) $\dfrac{2}{7} + \dfrac{6}{21} =$

6) $\dfrac{7}{8} + \dfrac{4}{12} =$

7) $\dfrac{5}{6} + \dfrac{8}{9} =$

8) $\dfrac{3}{5} + \dfrac{7}{15} =$

9) $\dfrac{6}{12} + \dfrac{4}{6} =$

10) $\dfrac{1}{6} + \dfrac{2}{6} =$

11) $\dfrac{1}{4} + \dfrac{1}{5} =$

12) $\dfrac{2}{3} + \dfrac{6}{9} =$

13) $\dfrac{4}{5} + \dfrac{6}{15} =$

14) $\dfrac{8}{21} + \dfrac{5}{7} =$

15) $\dfrac{1}{3} + \dfrac{7}{21} =$

16) $\dfrac{9}{16} + \dfrac{6}{8} =$

17) $\dfrac{1}{2} + \dfrac{9}{12} =$

18) $\dfrac{9}{10} + \dfrac{3}{5} =$

19) $\dfrac{2}{7} + \dfrac{3}{7} =$

20) $\dfrac{2}{3} + \dfrac{3}{4} =$

21) $\dfrac{3}{5} + \dfrac{4}{10} =$

22) $\dfrac{2}{16} + \dfrac{4}{8} =$

23) $\dfrac{8}{20} + \dfrac{8}{10} =$

24) $\dfrac{2}{6} + \dfrac{3}{12} =$

25) $\dfrac{4}{5} + \dfrac{5}{15} =$

26) $\dfrac{2}{7} + \dfrac{5}{7} =$

27) $\dfrac{5}{6} + \dfrac{1}{6} =$

28) $\dfrac{6}{20} + \dfrac{5}{10} =$

29) $\dfrac{8}{12} + \dfrac{3}{4} =$

30) $\dfrac{6}{7} + \dfrac{1}{4} =$

31) $\dfrac{3}{4} + \dfrac{7}{10} =$

32) $\dfrac{3}{5} + \dfrac{1}{5} =$

33) $\dfrac{5}{18} + \dfrac{7}{9} =$

34) $\dfrac{2}{3} + \dfrac{4}{5} =$

35) $\dfrac{7}{21} + \dfrac{3}{7} =$

36) $\dfrac{5}{6} + \dfrac{3}{9} =$

37) $\dfrac{3}{8} + \dfrac{2}{8} =$

38) $\dfrac{4}{8} + \dfrac{5}{8} =$

39) $\dfrac{4}{12} + \dfrac{1}{6} =$

40) $\dfrac{4}{6} + \dfrac{8}{12} =$

Adding Fractions

Day: **Time:**   **Score:**   /40

1) $\dfrac{9}{10} + \dfrac{2}{10} =$
2) $\dfrac{2}{8} + \dfrac{1}{8} =$
3) $\dfrac{3}{5} + \dfrac{1}{5} =$
4) $\dfrac{3}{5} + \dfrac{4}{5} =$

5) $\dfrac{7}{8} + \dfrac{3}{8} =$
6) $\dfrac{2}{9} + \dfrac{4}{6} =$
7) $\dfrac{3}{12} + \dfrac{3}{12} =$
8) $\dfrac{1}{5} + \dfrac{2}{3} =$

9) $\dfrac{2}{5} + \dfrac{4}{5} =$
10) $\dfrac{2}{3} + \dfrac{1}{3} =$
11) $\dfrac{2}{8} + \dfrac{4}{16} =$
12) $\dfrac{5}{8} + \dfrac{7}{8} =$

13) $\dfrac{1}{6} + \dfrac{4}{6} =$
14) $\dfrac{4}{6} + \dfrac{8}{12} =$
15) $\dfrac{5}{8} + \dfrac{4}{8} =$
16) $\dfrac{6}{8} + \dfrac{5}{16} =$

17) $\dfrac{7}{16} + \dfrac{1}{2} =$
18) $\dfrac{5}{9} + \dfrac{2}{9} =$
19) $\dfrac{5}{6} + \dfrac{1}{4} =$
20) $\dfrac{2}{8} + \dfrac{2}{16} =$

21) $\dfrac{1}{4} + \dfrac{8}{10} =$
22) $\dfrac{1}{4} + \dfrac{3}{4} =$
23) $\dfrac{7}{8} + \dfrac{9}{12} =$
24) $\dfrac{3}{5} + \dfrac{8}{15} =$

25) $\dfrac{1}{3} + \dfrac{2}{3} =$
26) $\dfrac{4}{16} + \dfrac{1}{2} =$
27) $\dfrac{4}{10} + \dfrac{4}{5} =$
28) $\dfrac{5}{8} + \dfrac{6}{16} =$

29) $\dfrac{6}{8} + \dfrac{3}{4} =$
30) $\dfrac{4}{8} + \dfrac{1}{2} =$
31) $\dfrac{1}{3} + \dfrac{1}{6} =$
32) $\dfrac{5}{6} + \dfrac{4}{6} =$

33) $\dfrac{2}{3} + \dfrac{3}{5} =$
34) $\dfrac{8}{14} + \dfrac{3}{28} =$
35) $\dfrac{1}{6} + \dfrac{1}{4} =$
36) $\dfrac{2}{3} + \dfrac{1}{3} =$

37) $\dfrac{1}{8} + \dfrac{1}{2} =$
38) $\dfrac{1}{2} + \dfrac{9}{12} =$
39) $\dfrac{5}{15} + \dfrac{3}{15} =$
40) $\dfrac{4}{6} + \dfrac{8}{18} =$

Adding Fractions

Day: **Time:**   **Score:**   /40

1) $\dfrac{7}{15} + \dfrac{9}{15} =$

2) $\dfrac{7}{20} + \dfrac{9}{20} =$

3) $\dfrac{3}{7} + \dfrac{3}{4} =$

4) $\dfrac{6}{8} + \dfrac{3}{16} =$

5) $\dfrac{6}{12} + \dfrac{3}{4} =$

6) $\dfrac{3}{8} + \dfrac{3}{4} =$

7) $\dfrac{5}{10} + \dfrac{4}{10} =$

8) $\dfrac{8}{30} + \dfrac{7}{30} =$

9) $\dfrac{2}{6} + \dfrac{1}{6} =$

10) $\dfrac{3}{5} + \dfrac{6}{15} =$

11) $\dfrac{9}{10} + \dfrac{4}{5} =$

12) $\dfrac{6}{7} + \dfrac{2}{3} =$

13) $\dfrac{7}{9} + \dfrac{6}{9} =$

14) $\dfrac{4}{20} + \dfrac{2}{20} =$

15) $\dfrac{1}{2} + \dfrac{4}{8} =$

16) $\dfrac{2}{8} + \dfrac{9}{12} =$

17) $\dfrac{1}{7} + \dfrac{2}{3} =$

18) $\dfrac{2}{6} + \dfrac{2}{12} =$

19) $\dfrac{5}{8} + \dfrac{4}{6} =$

20) $\dfrac{1}{3} + \dfrac{2}{3} =$

21) $\dfrac{3}{12} + \dfrac{8}{12} =$

22) $\dfrac{6}{15} + \dfrac{1}{3} =$

23) $\dfrac{5}{10} + \dfrac{4}{5} =$

24) $\dfrac{2}{3} + \dfrac{6}{7} =$

25) $\dfrac{1}{7} + \dfrac{2}{21} =$

26) $\dfrac{3}{8} + \dfrac{1}{4} =$

27) $\dfrac{5}{6} + \dfrac{4}{6} =$

28) $\dfrac{9}{20} + \dfrac{3}{20} =$

29) $\dfrac{6}{15} + \dfrac{3}{5} =$

30) $\dfrac{2}{8} + \dfrac{6}{8} =$

31) $\dfrac{5}{6} + \dfrac{4}{6} =$

32) $\dfrac{1}{4} + \dfrac{5}{20} =$

33) $\dfrac{3}{5} + \dfrac{2}{3} =$

34) $\dfrac{4}{5} + \dfrac{1}{3} =$

35) $\dfrac{3}{4} + \dfrac{2}{8} =$

36) $\dfrac{1}{3} + \dfrac{2}{3} =$

37) $\dfrac{4}{12} + \dfrac{6}{12} =$

38) $\dfrac{6}{12} + \dfrac{1}{6} =$

39) $\dfrac{5}{10} + \dfrac{3}{5} =$

40) $\dfrac{2}{12} + \dfrac{3}{8} =$

Subtracting Fractions

Day: **Time:**   **Score:** /40

1) $\dfrac{4}{5} - \dfrac{1}{3} =$

2) $\dfrac{4}{6} - \dfrac{1}{3} =$

3) $\dfrac{3}{8} - \dfrac{1}{8} =$

4) $\dfrac{5}{7} - \dfrac{1}{7} =$

5) $\dfrac{7}{8} - \dfrac{3}{8} =$

6) $\dfrac{7}{8} - \dfrac{4}{8} =$

7) $\dfrac{2}{3} - \dfrac{3}{5} =$

8) $\dfrac{4}{5} - \dfrac{1}{4} =$

9) $\dfrac{7}{8} - \dfrac{5}{8} =$

10) $\dfrac{4}{6} - \dfrac{4}{8} =$

11) $\dfrac{5}{6} - \dfrac{4}{6} =$

12) $\dfrac{3}{5} - \dfrac{3}{20} =$

13) $\dfrac{1}{2} - \dfrac{6}{18} =$

14) $\dfrac{6}{12} - \dfrac{1}{8} =$

15) $\dfrac{3}{4} - \dfrac{1}{10} =$

16) $\dfrac{8}{16} - \dfrac{3}{8} =$

17) $\dfrac{6}{12} - \dfrac{3}{8} =$

18) $\dfrac{5}{6} - \dfrac{2}{6} =$

19) $\dfrac{8}{12} - \dfrac{6}{18} =$

20) $\dfrac{3}{5} - \dfrac{8}{20} =$

21) $\dfrac{2}{10} - \dfrac{1}{20} =$

22) $\dfrac{4}{15} - \dfrac{1}{5} =$

23) $\dfrac{5}{7} - \dfrac{2}{3} =$

24) $\dfrac{6}{8} - \dfrac{1}{8} =$

25) $\dfrac{1}{4} - \dfrac{3}{12} =$

26) $\dfrac{4}{5} - \dfrac{1}{4} =$

27) $\dfrac{5}{6} - \dfrac{3}{12} =$

28) $\dfrac{5}{8} - \dfrac{2}{8} =$

29) $\dfrac{4}{6} - \dfrac{5}{12} =$

30) $\dfrac{3}{7} - \dfrac{3}{21} =$

31) $\dfrac{3}{5} - \dfrac{1}{5} =$

32) $\dfrac{8}{12} - \dfrac{1}{12} =$

33) $\dfrac{3}{15} - \dfrac{1}{5} =$

34) $\dfrac{7}{8} - \dfrac{6}{8} =$

35) $\dfrac{3}{5} - \dfrac{1}{5} =$

36) $\dfrac{6}{20} - \dfrac{1}{10} =$

37) $\dfrac{1}{5} - \dfrac{3}{15} =$

38) $\dfrac{4}{7} - \dfrac{6}{21} =$

39) $\dfrac{7}{8} - \dfrac{2}{8} =$

40) $\dfrac{3}{10} - \dfrac{1}{5} =$

Subtracting Fractions

Day:　　　　Time:　　　　Score:　　／40

1) $\dfrac{8}{20} - \dfrac{3}{20} =$　　2) $\dfrac{7}{9} - \dfrac{2}{18} =$　　3) $\dfrac{5}{6} - \dfrac{4}{6} =$　　4) $\dfrac{6}{7} - \dfrac{4}{7} =$

5) $\dfrac{1}{2} - \dfrac{2}{28} =$　　6) $\dfrac{4}{9} - \dfrac{2}{9} =$　　7) $\dfrac{4}{5} - \dfrac{4}{10} =$　　8) $\dfrac{1}{5} - \dfrac{3}{20} =$

9) $\dfrac{4}{5} - \dfrac{4}{10} =$　　10) $\dfrac{2}{3} - \dfrac{1}{5} =$　　11) $\dfrac{1}{5} - \dfrac{3}{15} =$　　12) $\dfrac{7}{8} - \dfrac{3}{16} =$

13) $\dfrac{5}{10} - \dfrac{7}{20} =$　　14) $\dfrac{6}{28} - \dfrac{3}{28} =$　　15) $\dfrac{2}{3} - \dfrac{1}{7} =$　　16) $\dfrac{4}{7} - \dfrac{3}{7} =$

17) $\dfrac{5}{6} - \dfrac{2}{6} =$　　18) $\dfrac{4}{5} - \dfrac{4}{15} =$　　19) $\dfrac{2}{7} - \dfrac{1}{7} =$　　20) $\dfrac{7}{8} - \dfrac{1}{8} =$

21) $\dfrac{2}{3} - \dfrac{1}{6} =$　　22) $\dfrac{4}{5} - \dfrac{2}{5} =$　　23) $\dfrac{7}{8} - \dfrac{3}{4} =$　　24) $\dfrac{7}{30} - \dfrac{4}{30} =$

25) $\dfrac{4}{12} - \dfrac{1}{6} =$　　26) $\dfrac{7}{8} - \dfrac{1}{2} =$　　27) $\dfrac{4}{8} - \dfrac{2}{8} =$　　28) $\dfrac{7}{8} - \dfrac{4}{16} =$

29) $\dfrac{4}{6} - \dfrac{1}{2} =$　　30) $\dfrac{2}{3} - \dfrac{4}{9} =$　　31) $\dfrac{5}{8} - \dfrac{2}{8} =$　　32) $\dfrac{1}{4} - \dfrac{1}{8} =$

33) $\dfrac{2}{5} - \dfrac{3}{10} =$　　34) $\dfrac{4}{7} - \dfrac{8}{21} =$　　35) $\dfrac{2}{3} - \dfrac{9}{21} =$　　36) $\dfrac{2}{3} - \dfrac{4}{7} =$

37) $\dfrac{8}{16} - \dfrac{3}{8} =$　　38) $\dfrac{3}{14} - \dfrac{1}{7} =$　　39) $\dfrac{8}{9} - \dfrac{5}{9} =$　　40) $\dfrac{5}{6} - \dfrac{4}{12} =$

Subtracting Fractions

Day: Time: Score: /40

1) $\dfrac{3}{7} - \dfrac{1}{4} =$

2) $\dfrac{2}{3} - \dfrac{6}{15} =$

3) $\dfrac{3}{4} - \dfrac{2}{6} =$

4) $\dfrac{2}{3} - \dfrac{1}{6} =$

5) $\dfrac{6}{10} - \dfrac{2}{5} =$

6) $\dfrac{5}{7} - \dfrac{2}{7} =$

7) $\dfrac{5}{15} - \dfrac{3}{10} =$

8) $\dfrac{1}{5} - \dfrac{2}{10} =$

9) $\dfrac{6}{8} - \dfrac{2}{8} =$

10) $\dfrac{6}{7} - \dfrac{2}{7} =$

11) $\dfrac{3}{5} - \dfrac{4}{15} =$

12) $\dfrac{6}{7} - \dfrac{5}{7} =$

13) $\dfrac{3}{4} - \dfrac{5}{8} =$

14) $\dfrac{6}{8} - \dfrac{1}{8} =$

15) $\dfrac{5}{12} - \dfrac{2}{12} =$

16) $\dfrac{3}{4} - \dfrac{2}{8} =$

17) $\dfrac{5}{8} - \dfrac{3}{12} =$

18) $\dfrac{5}{14} - \dfrac{5}{14} =$

19) $\dfrac{1}{5} - \dfrac{2}{15} =$

20) $\dfrac{1}{6} - \dfrac{1}{8} =$

21) $\dfrac{6}{7} - \dfrac{1}{4} =$

22) $\dfrac{8}{9} - \dfrac{7}{9} =$

23) $\dfrac{4}{6} - \dfrac{1}{6} =$

24) $\dfrac{6}{7} - \dfrac{4}{7} =$

25) $\dfrac{5}{9} - \dfrac{5}{18} =$

26) $\dfrac{3}{8} - \dfrac{1}{8} =$

27) $\dfrac{2}{6} - \dfrac{2}{8} =$

28) $\dfrac{3}{4} - \dfrac{5}{8} =$

29) $\dfrac{2}{5} - \dfrac{1}{3} =$

30) $\dfrac{4}{5} - \dfrac{3}{5} =$

31) $\dfrac{4}{7} - \dfrac{2}{7} =$

32) $\dfrac{2}{5} - \dfrac{1}{5} =$

33) $\dfrac{6}{10} - \dfrac{8}{20} =$

34) $\dfrac{8}{10} - \dfrac{2}{10} =$

35) $\dfrac{1}{12} - \dfrac{1}{12} =$

36) $\dfrac{1}{2} - \dfrac{1}{6} =$

37) $\dfrac{6}{8} - \dfrac{2}{12} =$

38) $\dfrac{6}{8} - \dfrac{4}{8} =$

39) $\dfrac{7}{16} - \dfrac{2}{8} =$

40) $\dfrac{8}{10} - \dfrac{7}{20} =$

Multiplying Fractions

Day: **Time:**   **Score:**   /40

1) $\dfrac{5}{18} \times \dfrac{2}{9} =$

2) $\dfrac{5}{16} \times \dfrac{7}{8} =$

3) $\dfrac{3}{7} \times \dfrac{2}{7} =$

4) $\dfrac{3}{8} \times \dfrac{5}{8} =$

5) $\dfrac{6}{8} \times \dfrac{1}{8} =$

6) $\dfrac{1}{4} \times \dfrac{4}{8} =$

7) $\dfrac{4}{10} \times \dfrac{4}{10} =$

8) $\dfrac{7}{15} \times \dfrac{2}{5} =$

9) $\dfrac{2}{6} \times \dfrac{5}{12} =$

10) $\dfrac{4}{5} \times \dfrac{5}{10} =$

11) $\dfrac{2}{6} \times \dfrac{3}{12} =$

12) $\dfrac{9}{12} \times \dfrac{3}{4} =$

13) $\dfrac{2}{8} \times \dfrac{4}{8} =$

14) $\dfrac{3}{5} \times \dfrac{7}{15} =$

15) $\dfrac{8}{9} \times \dfrac{8}{18} =$

16) $\dfrac{6}{8} \times \dfrac{7}{8} =$

17) $\dfrac{3}{4} \times \dfrac{3}{7} =$

18) $\dfrac{6}{15} \times \dfrac{2}{3} =$

19) $\dfrac{7}{14} \times \dfrac{8}{14} =$

20) $\dfrac{2}{12} \times \dfrac{2}{8} =$

21) $\dfrac{4}{8} \times \dfrac{6}{8} =$

22) $\dfrac{1}{6} \times \dfrac{6}{12} =$

23) $\dfrac{6}{12} \times \dfrac{3}{12} =$

24) $\dfrac{2}{6} \times \dfrac{1}{6} =$

25) $\dfrac{1}{10} \times \dfrac{4}{20} =$

26) $\dfrac{3}{21} \times \dfrac{5}{7} =$

27) $\dfrac{7}{10} \times \dfrac{2}{5} =$

28) $\dfrac{1}{8} \times \dfrac{2}{8} =$

29) $\dfrac{2}{7} \times \dfrac{4}{7} =$

30) $\dfrac{5}{14} \times \dfrac{1}{7} =$

31) $\dfrac{1}{5} \times \dfrac{2}{3} =$

32) $\dfrac{4}{6} \times \dfrac{1}{6} =$

33) $\dfrac{2}{8} \times \dfrac{4}{16} =$

34) $\dfrac{1}{5} \times \dfrac{9}{10} =$

35) $\dfrac{6}{7} \times \dfrac{5}{7} =$

36) $\dfrac{5}{10} \times \dfrac{3}{4} =$

37) $\dfrac{5}{6} \times \dfrac{2}{6} =$

38) $\dfrac{7}{20} \times \dfrac{1}{5} =$

39) $\dfrac{3}{4} \times \dfrac{1}{4} =$

40) $\dfrac{4}{15} \times \dfrac{3}{5} =$

Multiplying Fractions

Day: **Time:**   **Score:**   /40

1) $\dfrac{5}{9} \times \dfrac{2}{9} =$

2) $\dfrac{8}{12} \times \dfrac{4}{6} =$

3) $\dfrac{2}{16} \times \dfrac{2}{8} =$

4) $\dfrac{6}{7} \times \dfrac{3}{4} =$

5) $\dfrac{7}{8} \times \dfrac{5}{8} =$

6) $\dfrac{3}{4} \times \dfrac{5}{8} =$

7) $\dfrac{3}{8} \times \dfrac{2}{16} =$

8) $\dfrac{7}{20} \times \dfrac{2}{5} =$

9) $\dfrac{4}{5} \times \dfrac{8}{15} =$

10) $\dfrac{2}{8} \times \dfrac{6}{8} =$

11) $\dfrac{2}{7} \times \dfrac{9}{14} =$

12) $\dfrac{1}{2} \times \dfrac{5}{6} =$

13) $\dfrac{1}{6} \times \dfrac{5}{9} =$

14) $\dfrac{2}{3} \times \dfrac{6}{12} =$

15) $\dfrac{9}{21} \times \dfrac{4}{7} =$

16) $\dfrac{7}{8} \times \dfrac{3}{4} =$

17) $\dfrac{1}{6} \times \dfrac{7}{12} =$

18) $\dfrac{4}{18} \times \dfrac{4}{9} =$

19) $\dfrac{6}{7} \times \dfrac{3}{21} =$

20) $\dfrac{1}{2} \times \dfrac{3}{7} =$

21) $\dfrac{6}{8} \times \dfrac{2}{8} =$

22) $\dfrac{1}{7} \times \dfrac{3}{7} =$

23) $\dfrac{4}{8} \times \dfrac{3}{4} =$

24) $\dfrac{2}{15} \times \dfrac{1}{15} =$

25) $\dfrac{4}{6} \times \dfrac{2}{6} =$

26) $\dfrac{4}{8} \times \dfrac{7}{8} =$

27) $\dfrac{5}{8} \times \dfrac{7}{8} =$

28) $\dfrac{1}{4} \times \dfrac{3}{4} =$

29) $\dfrac{3}{4} \times \dfrac{6}{10} =$

30) $\dfrac{2}{5} \times \dfrac{2}{3} =$

31) $\dfrac{1}{2} \times \dfrac{4}{8} =$

32) $\dfrac{2}{15} \times \dfrac{2}{5} =$

33) $\dfrac{9}{15} \times \dfrac{4}{5} =$

34) $\dfrac{4}{15} \times \dfrac{1}{5} =$

35) $\dfrac{2}{12} \times \dfrac{2}{6} =$

36) $\dfrac{4}{5} \times \dfrac{5}{15} =$

37) $\dfrac{4}{6} \times \dfrac{1}{2} =$

38) $\dfrac{5}{8} \times \dfrac{1}{8} =$

39) $\dfrac{7}{9} \times \dfrac{4}{6} =$

40) $\dfrac{3}{8} \times \dfrac{7}{8} =$

Multiplying Fractions

Day: Time: Score: /40

1) $\dfrac{5}{8} \times \dfrac{3}{8} =$
2) $\dfrac{5}{15} \times \dfrac{3}{5} =$
3) $\dfrac{6}{15} \times \dfrac{1}{5} =$
4) $\dfrac{3}{4} \times \dfrac{6}{8} =$

5) $\dfrac{6}{15} \times \dfrac{4}{15} =$
6) $\dfrac{3}{4} \times \dfrac{9}{14} =$
7) $\dfrac{2}{10} \times \dfrac{5}{30} =$
8) $\dfrac{9}{15} \times \dfrac{8}{15} =$

9) $\dfrac{8}{20} \times \dfrac{4}{10} =$
10) $\dfrac{5}{8} \times \dfrac{2}{8} =$
11) $\dfrac{1}{4} \times \dfrac{2}{7} =$
12) $\dfrac{8}{12} \times \dfrac{1}{6} =$

13) $\dfrac{1}{6} \times \dfrac{2}{6} =$
14) $\dfrac{1}{4} \times \dfrac{4}{6} =$
15) $\dfrac{2}{8} \times \dfrac{4}{8} =$
16) $\dfrac{1}{4} \times \dfrac{4}{7} =$

17) $\dfrac{3}{10} \times \dfrac{6}{20} =$
18) $\dfrac{3}{12} \times \dfrac{7}{8} =$
19) $\dfrac{8}{18} \times \dfrac{6}{9} =$
20) $\dfrac{5}{12} \times \dfrac{3}{4} =$

21) $\dfrac{2}{10} \times \dfrac{4}{5} =$
22) $\dfrac{3}{20} \times \dfrac{3}{5} =$
23) $\dfrac{1}{4} \times \dfrac{3}{12} =$
24) $\dfrac{4}{8} \times \dfrac{2}{8} =$

25) $\dfrac{2}{7} \times \dfrac{4}{7} =$
26) $\dfrac{1}{7} \times \dfrac{5}{7} =$
27) $\dfrac{1}{4} \times \dfrac{2}{6} =$
28) $\dfrac{7}{8} \times \dfrac{3}{8} =$

29) $\dfrac{4}{7} \times \dfrac{6}{7} =$
30) $\dfrac{2}{6} \times \dfrac{1}{4} =$
31) $\dfrac{7}{18} \times \dfrac{5}{6} =$
32) $\dfrac{1}{6} \times \dfrac{5}{6} =$

33) $\dfrac{5}{8} \times \dfrac{7}{8} =$
34) $\dfrac{3}{10} \times \dfrac{8}{20} =$
35) $\dfrac{5}{14} \times \dfrac{4}{7} =$
36) $\dfrac{5}{15} \times \dfrac{4}{15} =$

37) $\dfrac{4}{12} \times \dfrac{4}{12} =$
38) $\dfrac{3}{5} \times \dfrac{4}{5} =$
39) $\dfrac{2}{14} \times \dfrac{3}{4} =$
40) $\dfrac{4}{12} \times \dfrac{5}{6} =$

Dividing Fractions

Day: Time: Score: /40

1) $\dfrac{6}{15} \div \dfrac{4}{5} =$

2) $\dfrac{5}{12} \div \dfrac{6}{12} =$

3) $\dfrac{7}{8} \div \dfrac{1}{2} =$

4) $\dfrac{3}{9} \div \dfrac{2}{6} =$

5) $\dfrac{5}{6} \div \dfrac{4}{6} =$

6) $\dfrac{3}{12} \div \dfrac{1}{2} =$

7) $\dfrac{1}{5} \div \dfrac{2}{5} =$

8) $\dfrac{2}{5} \div \dfrac{4}{5} =$

9) $\dfrac{3}{8} \div \dfrac{6}{8} =$

10) $\dfrac{1}{7} \div \dfrac{3}{7} =$

11) $\dfrac{4}{6} \div \dfrac{2}{6} =$

12) $\dfrac{1}{5} \div \dfrac{1}{10} =$

13) $\dfrac{4}{6} \div \dfrac{2}{6} =$

14) $\dfrac{8}{20} \div \dfrac{1}{5} =$

15) $\dfrac{3}{7} \div \dfrac{3}{14} =$

16) $\dfrac{6}{7} \div \dfrac{2}{7} =$

17) $\dfrac{5}{8} \div \dfrac{4}{8} =$

18) $\dfrac{2}{3} \div \dfrac{5}{15} =$

19) $\dfrac{4}{6} \div \dfrac{1}{6} =$

20) $\dfrac{4}{8} \div \dfrac{6}{12} =$

21) $\dfrac{5}{6} \div \dfrac{5}{12} =$

22) $\dfrac{1}{8} \div \dfrac{3}{8} =$

23) $\dfrac{1}{4} \div \dfrac{5}{8} =$

24) $\dfrac{3}{8} \div \dfrac{2}{12} =$

25) $\dfrac{1}{7} \div \dfrac{3}{7} =$

26) $\dfrac{4}{16} \div \dfrac{9}{16} =$

27) $\dfrac{2}{21} \div \dfrac{2}{21} =$

28) $\dfrac{3}{4} \div \dfrac{4}{5} =$

29) $\dfrac{2}{5} \div \dfrac{1}{5} =$

30) $\dfrac{5}{9} \div \dfrac{7}{18} =$

31) $\dfrac{3}{4} \div \dfrac{5}{7} =$

32) $\dfrac{4}{16} \div \dfrac{6}{8} =$

33) $\dfrac{3}{12} \div \dfrac{5}{6} =$

34) $\dfrac{5}{6} \div \dfrac{1}{8} =$

35) $\dfrac{9}{10} \div \dfrac{3}{4} =$

36) $\dfrac{6}{8} \div \dfrac{5}{8} =$

37) $\dfrac{1}{4} \div \dfrac{4}{5} =$

38) $\dfrac{4}{15} \div \dfrac{1}{5} =$

39) $\dfrac{1}{4} \div \dfrac{2}{8} =$

40) $\dfrac{6}{12} \div \dfrac{3}{12} =$

Dividing Fractions

Day: **Time:**   **Score:**   /40

1) $\dfrac{2}{10} \div \dfrac{1}{5} =$

2) $\dfrac{1}{7} \div \dfrac{3}{7} =$

3) $\dfrac{1}{5} \div \dfrac{2}{3} =$

4) $\dfrac{2}{5} \div \dfrac{3}{15} =$

5) $\dfrac{4}{6} \div \dfrac{4}{9} =$

6) $\dfrac{4}{5} \div \dfrac{1}{4} =$

7) $\dfrac{1}{10} \div \dfrac{3}{5} =$

8) $\dfrac{2}{7} \div \dfrac{8}{21} =$

9) $\dfrac{5}{6} \div \dfrac{1}{9} =$

10) $\dfrac{4}{7} \div \dfrac{8}{14} =$

11) $\dfrac{6}{7} \div \dfrac{2}{3} =$

12) $\dfrac{7}{10} \div \dfrac{3}{5} =$

13) $\dfrac{7}{12} \div \dfrac{5}{6} =$

14) $\dfrac{7}{20} \div \dfrac{7}{10} =$

15) $\dfrac{3}{5} \div \dfrac{4}{15} =$

16) $\dfrac{3}{15} \div \dfrac{4}{5} =$

17) $\dfrac{1}{14} \div \dfrac{5}{14} =$

18) $\dfrac{3}{5} \div \dfrac{2}{5} =$

19) $\dfrac{9}{14} \div \dfrac{3}{7} =$

20) $\dfrac{7}{14} \div \dfrac{1}{7} =$

21) $\dfrac{3}{8} \div \dfrac{1}{8} =$

22) $\dfrac{5}{10} \div \dfrac{3}{5} =$

23) $\dfrac{4}{7} \div \dfrac{5}{7} =$

24) $\dfrac{4}{12} \div \dfrac{5}{8} =$

25) $\dfrac{1}{8} \div \dfrac{6}{8} =$

26) $\dfrac{3}{5} \div \dfrac{2}{3} =$

27) $\dfrac{2}{6} \div \dfrac{7}{12} =$

28) $\dfrac{2}{8} \div \dfrac{6}{8} =$

29) $\dfrac{4}{5} \div \dfrac{7}{10} =$

30) $\dfrac{9}{10} \div \dfrac{4}{5} =$

31) $\dfrac{2}{15} \div \dfrac{5}{10} =$

32) $\dfrac{1}{2} \div \dfrac{7}{8} =$

33) $\dfrac{1}{10} \div \dfrac{8}{10} =$

34) $\dfrac{1}{8} \div \dfrac{7}{8} =$

35) $\dfrac{3}{12} \div \dfrac{2}{12} =$

36) $\dfrac{4}{6} \div \dfrac{1}{2} =$

37) $\dfrac{6}{21} \div \dfrac{3}{7} =$

38) $\dfrac{6}{7} \div \dfrac{3}{4} =$

39) $\dfrac{2}{8} \div \dfrac{4}{6} =$

40) $\dfrac{4}{5} \div \dfrac{2}{10} =$

Dividing Fractions

Day:　　　Time:　　　Score:　　/40

1) $\dfrac{2}{6} \div \dfrac{5}{6} =$ 　　2) $\dfrac{4}{6} \div \dfrac{5}{6} =$ 　　3) $\dfrac{1}{5} \div \dfrac{3}{15} =$ 　　4) $\dfrac{5}{8} \div \dfrac{3}{4} =$

5) $\dfrac{4}{5} \div \dfrac{7}{15} =$ 　　6) $\dfrac{5}{6} \div \dfrac{6}{8} =$ 　　7) $\dfrac{4}{5} \div \dfrac{1}{5} =$ 　　8) $\dfrac{1}{3} \div \dfrac{2}{7} =$

9) $\dfrac{7}{18} \div \dfrac{3}{12} =$ 　　10) $\dfrac{5}{8} \div \dfrac{3}{4} =$ 　　11) $\dfrac{3}{8} \div \dfrac{1}{8} =$ 　　12) $\dfrac{7}{16} \div \dfrac{3}{16} =$

13) $\dfrac{6}{15} \div \dfrac{3}{5} =$ 　　14) $\dfrac{4}{5} \div \dfrac{3}{5} =$ 　　15) $\dfrac{5}{6} \div \dfrac{1}{12} =$ 　　16) $\dfrac{3}{16} \div \dfrac{9}{16} =$

17) $\dfrac{3}{7} \div \dfrac{2}{28} =$ 　　18) $\dfrac{5}{8} \div \dfrac{5}{12} =$ 　　19) $\dfrac{6}{7} \div \dfrac{1}{7} =$ 　　20) $\dfrac{3}{5} \div \dfrac{7}{15} =$

21) $\dfrac{2}{8} \div \dfrac{3}{4} =$ 　　22) $\dfrac{2}{7} \div \dfrac{6}{7} =$ 　　23) $\dfrac{2}{5} \div \dfrac{3}{5} =$ 　　24) $\dfrac{5}{16} \div \dfrac{3}{8} =$

25) $\dfrac{3}{4} \div \dfrac{3}{28} =$ 　　26) $\dfrac{4}{6} \div \dfrac{2}{6} =$ 　　27) $\dfrac{8}{12} \div \dfrac{1}{2} =$ 　　28) $\dfrac{1}{6} \div \dfrac{2}{3} =$

29) $\dfrac{2}{8} \div \dfrac{5}{8} =$ 　　30) $\dfrac{5}{8} \div \dfrac{1}{6} =$ 　　31) $\dfrac{1}{5} \div \dfrac{2}{5} =$ 　　32) $\dfrac{6}{7} \div \dfrac{2}{7} =$

33) $\dfrac{6}{15} \div \dfrac{1}{15} =$ 　　34) $\dfrac{4}{9} \div \dfrac{5}{9} =$ 　　35) $\dfrac{6}{7} \div \dfrac{1}{7} =$ 　　36) $\dfrac{5}{12} \div \dfrac{4}{8} =$

37) $\dfrac{5}{8} \div \dfrac{6}{8} =$ 　　38) $\dfrac{1}{5} \div \dfrac{5}{10} =$ 　　39) $\dfrac{4}{8} \div \dfrac{7}{8} =$ 　　40) $\dfrac{4}{15} \div \dfrac{2}{5} =$

Word Problems

12 worksheets
10 problems per sheet

William. Education

Word Problems

1) Allen has 99 small nails to hang 23 signs. If each sign requires 4 small nails, how many small nails will be left over after hanging the signs?

2) Jane is 11 years old. She has friends who are 9, 7, 9, and 10 years old. How much older than Jane would someone be if all the ages were added together?

3) In math class Dick added up the numbers 3, 6, 9, and 13. After he was done he subtracted 4. What was the final number for Dick?

4) You need to solve 10 writing problems to pass a test on Tuesday. If you have 1 minute to take the test, how many seconds can you spend on each question?

5) You have 6 small blue containers. If each one can hold 6 thumbtacks, how many thumbtacks will you need to fill your containers?

6) During a trip to the forest on Saturday Debra collected 46 ants. She wants to give them to her 4 friends from Oregon. Before she divides the ants up, 14 get away. How many ants will each friend get?

7) Wednesday's band practice starts at 3:15 and is 9 blocks from Allen's house. If Allen can walk each block in 5 minutes, what's the latest he can leave in order to get there on time?

8) Each girl in 1st grade can collect 15 box tops per week. If there are 8 girls in the 1st grade, how many box tops can be collected in 5 weeks?

9) It's a sunny day and Toby is filling up his bookcase which holds 85 model airplanes. Toby has already put 56 model airplanes away. How many model airplanes does he still have to put away?

10) After dinner Lisa wrote 18 sentences for her awesome story, but forgot that she wasn't allowed to have more than 11 sentences. How many sentences does she need to remove?

Word Problems

1) Your ping-pong class has 13 great kids. You need to create 3 teams of the same size to play games. How many kids won't be able to play games?

2) You need to solve 15 hard problems to pass a test on Tuesday. If you have 1 minute to take the test, how many seconds can you spend on each question?

3) John wrote an exciting story about cats. The story has 110 sentences and each page can contain 10 sentences. How many pages will the story be?

4) During a trip to Wyoming on Saturday Tammy collected 52 insects. She wants to give them to her 6 friends from Oregon. Before she divides the insects up, 16 get away. How many insects will each friend get?

5) Wendy needs to divide $28 in new quarters into 7 rolls? How many quarters will be in each roll?

6) Tuesday's soccer practice starts at 1:15 and is 7 blocks from Allen's house. If Allen can walk each block in 5 minutes, what's the latest he can leave in order to get there on time?

7) You can walk 12 feet in 20 seconds. How many seconds will it take you to walk 72 feet from your bedroom to your basement?

8) Nancy is chosen to inspect spoons to make sure they work. For each 14 she inspects she finds 1 that is bad. If Nancy finds 5 bad spoons, how many are good?

9) Nathan had 38 tin bottles that he wanted to share with his history class. He gave Debra 3, Larry 9, and Nancy 13. How many bottles did Nathan have left?

10) Before lunch Jared wrote 14 sentences for his short story, but forgot that he wasn't allowed to have more than 10 sentences. How many sentences does he need to remove?

Word Problems

1) Mack has 110 large nails to hang 24 pictures. If each picture requires 4 large nails, how many large nails will be left over after hanging the pictures?

2) Marie is 9 years old. She has friends who are 12, 9, 8, and 12 years old. How much older than Marie would someone be if all the ages were added together?

3) You need to solve 5 writing problems to pass a test on Thursday. If you have 1 minute to take the test, how many seconds can you spend on each question?

4) Mandy wrote an short story about turtles. The story has 75 sentences and each page can contain 10 sentences. How many pages will the story be?

5) You have 3 small clay jars. If each one can hold 5 pennies, how many pennies will you need to fill your jars?

6) During a trip to the lake on Tuesday Katie collected 46 butterflies. She wants to give them to her 4 friends from the country. Before she divides the butterflies up, 14 get away. How many butterflies will each friend get?

7) Mary lives 4 miles from camp. If she can run each mile in 8 minutes and leaves at 1:30, what time will she arrive?

8) Thursday's soccer practice starts at 2:00 and is 4 blocks from Andy's house. If Andy can walk each block in 5 minutes, what's the latest he can leave in order to get there on time?

9) Eric wants to buy 11 red pencils. Each pencil costs 25 cents. How much money does Eric need to buy the pencils?

10) Steve had 29 tin glasses that he wanted to share with his math class. He gave Mary 6, Neal 7, and Barb 14. How many glasses did Steve have left?

Word Problems

1) Barney has 65 push pins to hang 15 signs. If each sign requires 4 push pins, how many push pins will be left over after hanging the signs?

2) You need to solve 6 science problems to pass a test on Wednesday. If you have 1 minute to take the test, how many seconds can you spend on each question?

3) Wednesday's basketball practice starts at 1:15 and is 7 blocks from Allen's house. If Allen can walk each block in 5 minutes, what's the latest he can leave in order to get there on time?

4) Each kid in 1st grade can collect 5 stickers per week. If there are 5 kids in the 1st grade, how many stickers can be collected in 3 weeks?

5) Mary is chosen to inspect spoons to make sure they work. For each 24 she inspects she finds 3 that are bad. If Mary finds 9 bad spoons, how many are good?

6) It's a cloudy day and Michael is filling up his basement which holds 50 books. Michael has already put 32 books away. How many books does he still have to put away?

7) Norman had 60 tall bottles that he wanted to share with his gym class. He gave Susan 7, Mark 14, and Renee 23. How many bottles did Norman have left?

8) After a field trip Bill wrote 14 sentences for his dramatic story, but forgot that he wasn't allowed to have more than 10 sentences. How many sentences does he need to remove?

9) Nancy is 14 years old. She has friends who are 11, 9, 12, and 9 years old. How much older than Nancy would someone be if all the ages were added together?

10) In math class Allen added up the numbers 5, 8, 14, and 22. After he was done he subtracted 8. What was the final number for Allen?

Word Problems

1) Allen has 99 large nails to hang 23 pictures. If each picture requires 4 large nails, how many large nails will be left over after hanging the pictures?

2) Marie is 10 years old. She has friends who are 9, 7, 8, and 11 years old. How much older than Marie would someone be if all the ages were added together?

3) In math class Chuck added up the numbers 6, 8, 13, and 16. After he was done he subtracted 9. What was the final number for Chuck?

4) You have 3 small plastic jars. If each one can hold 5 thumbtacks, how many thumbtacks will you need to fill your jars?

5) During a trip to the lake on Saturday Barb collected 52 flies. She wants to give them to her 6 friends from gym class. Before she divides the flies up, 16 get away. How many flies will each friend get?

6) Carol lives 5 miles from camp. If she can skip each mile in 9 minutes and leaves at 2:00, what time will she arrive?

7) Todd wants to order pizza for the birthday party on Tuesday. Each pizza has 5 slices. If the 10 kids at the party each eat 4 slices, how many pizzas should Todd order?

8) Wednesday's soccer practice starts at 1:15 and is 7 blocks from Allen's house. If Allen can walk each block in 5 minutes, what's the latest he can leave in order to get there on time?

9) James wants to buy 12 great rulers. Each ruler costs 33 cents. How much money does James need to buy the rulers?

10) Nick had 40 purple glasses that he wanted to share with his math class. He gave Laura 8, Al 12, and Jean 15. How many glasses did Nick have left?

Word Problems

1) A castle in London has 3 paintings of waterfalls. Assuming that each painting is 3 inches wide and 2.5 inches tall, what is the length of all the sides of the paintings in inches?

2) Todd finds $111.22 while visiting Maine. He wants to distribute his money evenly to his 7 friends. If $15.81 is lost on the way back to Seattle, how much money will each of his 7 friends get when he returns?

3) Wanda measures the length of 12 blue pencils. If the total of all lengths is 53.4 inches, what is the average length of a single pencil?

4) Steve drove a red car 869 miles to Oregon last spring and used a total of 50 gallons of gasoline. What was the average miles driven per gallon of gasoline?

5) During Mason's summer barbecue a total of 21 strawberry pies were made. Each person received 1/2 of a pie. How many people were at the barbecue?

6) You want to purchase 20 valuable inches of cord at the store. The regular cost for cord is $25.40 per inch, but next Tuesday a sale will give you 9% off the total price. How much can you purchase the cord for on Tuesday?

7) Landon had 760 tiny blue marbles. He gave his cousin Alice 35% of them. How many marbles did Landon keep for himself?

8) Leslie wants to buy a radio that costs $225.00. If she can save $45.00 a week working at the coffee shop, how many weeks will Leslie have to work in order to buy the radio?

9) The temperature one spring day was 102 degrees. Starting at 1:20 PM the temperature drops 0.5 degrees per minute. What temperature will it be at 1:55 PM?

10) Goodness! You find out your pipe is leaking 24 pints of water every 4 hours. After 2 hours, how many gallons of water will have leaked from the pipe?

Word Problems

1) Corby finds $99.85 while visiting Florida. He wants to distribute his money evenly to his 5 friends. If $21.00 is lost on the way back to Seattle, how much money will each of his 5 friends get when he returns?

2) Mark measures the length of 10 green books. If the total of all lengths is 66.1 inches, what is the average length of a single book?

3) The soccer coach bought 10 mushroom pizzas for the gang. If each pizza had 6 slices and 3/4 of all slices are eaten, how many slices were left over?

4) John drove a green car 864 miles to Oregon last summer and used a total of 40 gallons of gasoline. What was the average miles driven per gallon of gasoline?

5) During Carson's summer social a total of 23 strawberry pies were made. Each person received 1/4 of a pie. How many people were at the social?

6) You want to purchase 15 valuable feet of rope at the store. The regular cost for rope is $11.20 per foot, but next Tuesday a sale will give you 5% off the total price. How much can you purchase the rope for on Tuesday?

7) All girls were asked what their favorite subject was. If 3/5 of the girls liked biology and 3/8 liked drama, what fraction did not like biology and drama?

8) Tyler had 464 small brown marbles. He gave his cousin Joy 25% of them. How many marbles did Tyler keep for himself?

9) Ellen can throw 72 pitches in 2 minutes. How many pitches can Ellen throw in 45 seconds?

10) The stockroom has 74 gray pails of water in the front room. Workers are able to haul off 30 pails every 3 days. How many pails will still remain in the front room after 4 days?

Word Problems

1) Todd finds $105.28 while visiting Maine. He wants to distribute his money evenly to his 5 friends. If $12.18 is lost on the way back to Sacramento, how much money will each of his 5 friends get when he returns?

2) The volleyball coach bought 12 sausage pizzas for the party. If each pizza had 4 slices and 2/3 of all slices are eaten, how many slices were left over?

3) Anna has $1,650 to buy supplies for making a new building. If she spends 1/2 of her money during the first 7 weeks of construction, how much money will she still have to spend on supplies?

4) Barb likes peanut candy bars and wants to share 3/4 of them with her friends. If she gives one to each of her 18 friends, how many candy bars will she need before starting to share?

5) During Matt's summer social a total of 66 watermelons were made. Each person received 1/2 of a watermelon. How many people were at the social?

6) All girls were asked what their favorite subject was. If 2/5 of the girls liked algebra and 2/5 liked social studies, what fraction did not like algebra and social studies?

7) Sam had 708 small yellow marbles. He gave his cousin Joy 25% of them. How many marbles did Sam keep for himself?

8) Sean can throw 126 curve balls in 7 minutes. How many curve balls can Sean throw in 30 seconds?

9) The outlet store on Farm Lane has a expensive scarf for $53. The scarf price goes up 20% next week. How much money will you save if you buy the scarf today?

10) You decide to start a small craft project using green string. You need to cut 12 pieces of string, each 13 inches long. How many feet of string do you need to purchase for the project?

Word Problems

1) A museum in England has 3 paintings of climbers. Assuming that each painting is 3 inches wide and 2.5 inches tall, what is the length of all the sides of the paintings in inches?

2) Craig measures the length of 8 white hats. If the total of all lengths is 107.6 inches, what is the average length of a single hat?

3) Reagan has $400 to buy supplies for making a small office. If he spends 3/4 of his money during the first 3 weeks of construction, how much money will he still have to spend on supplies?

4) Holly drove a yellow car 783 miles to Maine last fall and used a total of 50 gallons of gasoline. What was the average miles driven per gallon of gasoline?

5) Levi had 755 small orange marbles. He gave his cousin Maria 20% of them. How many marbles did Levi keep for himself?

6) Loren wants to buy a chair that costs $112.95. If he can save $12.55 a week working at the store, how many weeks will Loren have to work in order to buy the chair?

7) Justin can throw 64 fast pitches in 4 minutes. How many pitches can Justin throw in 15 seconds?

8) The store has 65 black barrels of water in the front room. Workers are able to haul off 30 barrels every 2 days. How many barrels will still remain in the front room after 2 days?

9) The outlet store on Wood Lane has a expensive blender for $50. The blender price goes up 5% next week. How much money will you save if you buy the blender today?

10) During a sunny spring day you find 34 large ants in the back yard. You want to give 7/8 of the ants to your friends. If 2 ants escape before you can share, how many ants will you give away?

Word Problems

1) A house in Sweden has 7 paintings of mountains. Assuming that each painting is 7 inches wide and 4 inches tall, what is the length of all the sides of the paintings in inches?

2) The weightlifting coach bought 12 seafood pizzas for the players. If each pizza had 4 slices and 2/3 of all slices are eaten, how many slices were left over?

3) Anna has $1,600 to buy supplies for making a new shelter. If she spends 1/2 of her money during the first 6 weeks of construction, how much money will she still have to spend on supplies?

4) Riley had 780 small yellow marbles. He gave his cousin Alice 40% of them. How many marbles did Riley keep for himself?

5) Debra wants to buy a cell phone that costs $420.50. If she can save $42.05 a week working at the movie theater, how many weeks will Debra have to work in order to buy the cell phone?

6) The building has 68 white barrels of salt in the side room. Workers are able to haul off 25 barrels every 2 days. How many barrels will still remain in the side room after 4 days?

7) The temperature one summer day was 102 degrees. Starting at 1:20 PM the temperature drops 0.5 degrees per minute. What temperature will it be at 1:55 PM?

8) Incredible! You find out your faucet is leaking 16 pints of water every 2 hours. After 3 hours, how many gallons of water will have leaked from the faucet?

9) Basketball practice is 10 blocks away and starts at 1:30 PM. If Stacy can walk each block in 5 minutes, what time does Stacy need to leave in order to arrive 5 minutes early?

10) Preparing to make 11 white shawls you discover each one will require 3.5 square yards of material. If each square yard of material costs $6.50, how much will it cost to make all the shawls?

Answer Key

Page1

82	86	117	96	96
90	89	146	89	75
125	60	185	82	167
76	63	96	122	44
98	95	137	98	120
75	86	71	74	178

Page2

115	136	81	154	79
111	182	64	51	143
140	75	132	151	68
70	87	154	88	89
141	23	145	127	75
178	74	118	97	172

Page3

69	143	41	163	105
139	157	29	120	122
172	151	147	127	83
135	91	114	140	124
80	180	74	90	168
66	86	62	180	164

Page4

135	116	115	143	101
50	127	121	188	105
47	78	130	66	113
54	172	146	78	111
116	107	129	138	85
75	123	157	135	149

Page5

1363	595	602	1017	687
1038	1034	649	867	803
1322	1353	688	815	679
670	1037	1059	1408	1381
1106	1285	800	507	1290
985	1306	272	1462	1374

Page6

1149	924	1743	1237	938
1592	1093	320	1026	1159
247	1389	1885	925	1233
1542	1391	1427	1390	1145
445	845	752	1493	860
821	1065	957	214	1528

Page7

1063	922	929	890	1085
1115	990	612	465	1714
1556	1498	1202	706	828
1206	504	988	1898	1115
1641	1077	1242	984	1485
619	1486	915	1860	1782

Page8

1662	1079	1507	1497	512
1387	1231	1731	1139	1434
440	727	1069	1433	1359
1059	1387	732	609	939
1237	1537	1539	1289	1018
1055	912	463	1002	745

Page9

9416	16118	10845	7639	16643
16288	16817	17555	16077	12071
8231	18067	8419	13993	9189
13407	13971	9696	11349	8931
10666	11209	10952	8223	10988
9442	15325	16336	16573	12326

Page10

9982	8154	11353	14271	14374
14532	11603	5525	10479	17984
8810	12584	3988	13555	15308
15574	8055	12375	6318	6384
11422	11395	7742	8714	15260
11532	8722	13401	7440	12556

Page11

10966	9356	6620	11043	8526
6959	10727	9112	5041	8730
8569	11798	12699	14418	8647
12116	9890	11918	7330	5963
13949	15695	16877	14264	7289
5673	6363	9418	12622	13879

Page12

14258	9112	10956	17915	6253
18616	15842	13015	11058	14136
2781	4670	9245	10706	7568
17168	13637	10631	10105	11680
14675	10827	8600	15159	5374
11340	17985	12371	5740	13594

Page13

47	17	1	3	10
14	18	12	17	19
29	35	59	12	13
21	31	47	31	3
36	2	1	1	13
13	41	3	55	33

Page14

15	13	1	5	16
16	1	5	8	32
75	32	59	32	36
5	6	12	43	7
5	30	13	62	20
11	6	26	19	19

Page15

37	6	14	33	10
42	48	30	6	5
0	2	2	15	34
26	44	2	10	61
3	64	1	18	7
33	3	14	8	15

Page16

60	21	1	66	28
26	20	5	4	25
5	1	9	68	12
23	40	9	11	11
1	76	11	18	25
3	5	42	62	52

Page17

30	126	421	239	146
103	649	79	197	505
84	161	563	100	154
302	338	8	207	17
266	168	184	657	111
466	636	644	589	34

Page18

158	277	301	47	41
558	255	73	378	382
184	281	130	225	5
406	23	5	469	7
281	103	239	632	221
128	338	695	153	19

Page19

39	689	627	492	495
89	575	3	25	130
400	27	269	72	218
574	31	129	35	25
258	225	272	80	132
176	414	520	297	66

Page20

253	604	325	452	13
417	238	263	353	56
262	197	177	270	212
137	476	130	264	120
121	11	124	15	39
160	454	504	362	9

Page21

3454	6456	3886	1496	93
4536	3196	2093	8627	518
1415	459	882	758	2189
1878	556	7809	907	112
8065	1139	2393	1284	3339
1713	139	508	1876	700

Page22

3399	1959	592	72	4460
643	928	1028	1723	561
784	323	2350	1242	5852
2012	2267	1506	1082	6826
86	5532	791	2700	1528
241	465	4280	6385	626

Page23

568	1559	3046	2733	2611
1550	4169	2	2258	1968
3006	1636	1763	1199	6587
658	832	5263	1097	563
1952	666	62	5003	93
1694	1298	779	44	3323

Page24

1067	307	4367	2147	1464
5418	877	22	78	28
2329	1476	2436	546	4168
1604	3109	945	2998	4004
2453	3811	5805	989	972
3388	980	847	2778	4693

Page25

234	51	93	184	640
456	623	60	225	312
324	176	395	301	384
164	819	410	306	188
128	630	63	837	582
469	308	90	135	123

Page26

208	423	36	232	231
44	568	259	178	455
336	126	470	112	136
78	115	264	504	333
712	305	76	720	168
88	392	66	285	40

Page27

288	70	186	568	480
325	776	215	765	208
261	504	120	528	112
184	256	455	378	39
305	384	396	147	69
504	292	105	96	168

Page28

324	228	744	160	324
405	248	128	222	376
189	240	180	36	344
92	290	66	324	264
222	99	665	56	54
351	124	231	312	180

Page29

3360	6900	1596	5980	2067
768	2385	4452	2730	2200
490	4324	946	2650	2576
860	5580	972	7138	1443
680	2511	540	460	4732
696	2080	990	3071	2352

Page30

8536	1472	5336	8736	2808
4864	4984	2368	510	3264
140	4094	7189	1488	1843
4508	976	3234	132	2774
3550	1260	6216	2280	2982
2842	616	8064	5694	4800

Page31

2769	3081	3600	649	1258
1332	1219	2401	6150	4136
5005	330	5680	3315	3060
700	3080	1224	6808	4005
3658	6160	1596	1980	6080
6318	169	1743	990	1674

Page32

5184	1540	3445	3111	3182
4224	5100	644	2442	5208
1560	2418	3224	6142	5040
1224	2691	1120	1647	5412
805	1254	2250	646	1846
6175	2720	833	3692	90

Page33

145782	373919	238377	520970	230698
775056	140070	556325	153924	315375
597895	99050	54737	132327	486948
434985	806548	773128	147987	231332
581330	181720	128148	175820	315950
68470	267633	543585	340531	183360

Page34

394250	265864	590205	362000	636548
235008	363720	578162	183960	476484
319894	677104	220010	720020	156404
152350	180930	489800	161236	451815
283269	431640	738794	246036	285824
481380	418132	248472	137379	197181

Page35

275726	170500	210380	308066	345450
79328	236602	239360	478962	75428
371790	332080	73308	837902	81375
244731	154546	126869	113696	220871
212197	331508	227164	81252	253759
54648	250305	535575	167562	126991

Page36

472736	207718	337696	195360	339915
198650	123366	501600	206580	273808
39861	553248	245410	497854	123420
551985	188496	82236	94400	122988
225203	272636	392873	121031	558090
404430	213150	202216	427908	173032

Page37

6R1	9R4	12	2R1	10R3
15R2	5R1	24R1	11R2	17R2
19R3	8R5	21R2	12	15
16R1	7R1	6R1	8	11R3
4R1	17	15R2	8R4	2R1
4R2	10R2	5R3	8	11R4
6R5	36R1	17R3	24R2	6R1
11R2	16	9R1	3	17

Page38

14	48	11R2	16R3	15R3
12	12R2	33	10	4R1
12R1	3R2	4R4	17R3	9R3
24	4R2	7R2	6	13R2
11	6R4	7	14R2	11R5
9R6	20R1	25R1	5R2	21R2
3R3	8	9R6	35R1	6R6
22R1	7R5	12R2	8R3	13R2

Page39

12R2	26R2	15R1	3R5	20R1
30R2	13R3	11R4	15R2	10R3
21R1	19	6R4	3R4	5R1
3R1	1R4	15	3R6	13R5
15R1	34	2R2	12R6	13R3
9	2R1	4R2	2	8
5R1	19R1	2R2	9R3	5R3
13R5	5R2	10R6	38	10R2

Page40

12R5	15R1	39R1	1R5	10R1
8	13R1	4R3	46R1	13R4
6R2	19R2	10R1	24R1	11
8	10R2	14	7R4	7R2
10	2R4	1R6	6R3	12R5
22	13R1	15R1	32	9R1
9R6	5R4	12R2	21	3R3
14R4	22R1	9R3	6R5	2R4

Page41

57R3	90R2	256R1	110R3	207
18R7	118R1	84R3	34R2	113R5
244R1	116	211R3	105R3	131R2
67R2	63	81R4	122R1	33R2
50R1	289R1	133	57	107R3
84R4	159R2	153R4	234	136R3
45R1	30R2	77R6	40R3	38R1
187R3	167R2	213	70	129R1

Page42

54R5	43R2	87R1	162R1	127R1
42R1	28R4	50R7	182R1	45R4
228	241	140R1	29R3	116R1
113R2	36R2	150R4	142R1	128R2
81R2	26R6	45R1	43R6	311R2
84R2	243R1	112R1	316R1	99R2
30R4	232R2	122	164R1	16R3
119R2	54R1	86R2	191R2	49R6

Page43

448	85R3	199	427R1	137R2
92R6	49R3	383	87R1	64R1
135R2	24R5	22R1	24R1	66R6
62R2	65	346R1	45R5	96R2
156R2	109R2	89R5	59R2	31R1
138	30R1	74R3	33R6	33R3
197R3	266R1	271	265	104R4
44R4	98R1	55R5	95R4	132

Page44

40R3	35R1	280	398	30R7
85R5	29R2	27R3	49R1	179R2
18R6	26R4	155R2	18R4	100R1
124R4	83R2	31R4	104R2	59R1
66R1	265R1	109	97R3	77R3
93R1	120R2	14R6	116	165R2
92	80	107	45R3	165R1
50R1	41R1	107R4	62R3	164R3

Page45

10R5	3R56	4R29	16R11	15R43
1R18	11R13	10R1	7R1	9R6
13R38	8R13	4R41	22R25	7R2
6R16	42R6	16R5	13R11	40R2
1R81	3R30	9R66	15R51	11R62
34R13	20R23	5R54	32R24	14R11
6R36	45R6	33R2	5R9	7R87
17R19	46R11	1R7	13R21	6R3

Page46

27R27	8R10	1R3	10R16	14R6
18R27	2R14	5R82	9R14	7R52
12R14	7R25	7R19	26R13	20R38
18R46	10R15	82	6R27	7R62
2R71	20R27	24R18	10R53	5R10
6R17	10R38	2R37	3R80	22R6
50R2	16R3	2R18	11R31	2R26
12R43	25R4	8R81	10R15	7R56

Page47

10R31	7R55	10R4	81R1	14R20
8R21	3R35	5R70	10R29	15R52
4R89	27R25	3R8	17R17	34R19
1R71	9R1	2R52	21R5	10R14
9R35	10R25	15R14	3R55	2R30
2R92	8R22	7R15	25R14	35R14
14R27	28R4	8R45	7R69	5R76
24R25	4R41	8R72	69R5	5R22

Page48

15R37	2R10	16R9	23R30	12R29
14R15	30R9	6R46	4R22	7R15
9R61	21R7	1R35	4R40	6R20
20R13	3R7	31R2	6R8	9R7
3R18	9R23	79	24R30	3R4
9	62R9	5R18	13R50	7R18
4R60	5R34	30R24	14R1	5R46
5R28	5R64	8R14	10R23	5R23

Page49

258R28	24R10	34R37	110R4	580R2
126R37	91R47	117R7	72R38	108R64
413R5	842R4	26R12	12R77	121R35
26R42	119R22	61R37	302R2	128R13
156R34	233R3	153R4	141R61	388R16
57R6	172R12	116R6	95R40	58R58
107R59	726R9	54R14	53R37	194R47
79R20	85R5	67R32	66R4	78R42

Page50

221R36	74R30	110R35	291R12	19R18
142R45	47R15	54R24	33R80	166R2
203	116R11	74R81	404R15	108R1
45R32	132R38	117R58	127R3	60R79
181R3	64R55	95R9	94R14	209
71R16	314R20	41R23	110R40	739R1
128R19	108R6	18R1	116R44	38R8
40R68	275R11	164R1	110R38	162R3

Page51

124R39	295R18	138R24	71R21	72R27
43R77	119R15	110R82	57R35	141R16
21R30	576R1	83R25	64R62	115R50
133R10	19R21	25R45	103R18	104R10
42R21	99R59	192R3	44R39	141R58
21R84	138R7	52R73	100R66	27R23
144R7	28R36	145R12	170R46	156R22
27R62	459R10	216R24	114R53	116R59

Page52

2/3	1	10/7	19/21
4/7	29/24	31/18	16/15
7/6	1/2	9/20	4/3
6/5	23/21	2/3	21/16
5/4	3/2	5/7	17/12
1	5/8	6/5	7/12
17/15	1	1	4/5
17/12	31/28	29/20	4/5
19/18	22/15	16/21	7/6
5/8	9/8	1/2	4/3

Page53

11/10	3/8	4/5	7/5
5/4	8/9	1/2	13/15
6/5	1	1/2	3/2
5/6	4/3	9/8	17/16
15/16	7/9	13/12	3/8
21/20	1	13/8	17/15
1	3/4	6/5	1
3/2	1	1/2	3/2
19/15	19/28	5/12	1
5/8	5/4	8/15	10/9

Page54

16/15	4/5	33/28	15/16
5/4	9/8	9/10	1/2
1/2	1	17/10	32/21
13/9	3/10	1	1
17/21	1/2	31/24	1
11/12	11/15	13/10	32/21
5/21	5/8	3/2	3/5
1	1	3/2	1/2
19/15	17/15	1	1
5/6	2/3	11/10	13/24

Page55

7/15	1/3	1/4	4/7
1/2	3/8	1/15	11/20
1/4	1/6	1/6	9/20
1/6	3/8	13/20	1/8
1/8	1/2	1/3	1/5
3/20	1/15	1/21	5/8
0	11/20	7/12	3/8
1/4	2/7	2/5	7/12
0	1/8	2/5	1/5
0	2/7	5/8	1/10

Page56

1/4	2/3	1/6	2/7
3/7	2/9	2/5	1/20
2/5	7/15	0	11/16
3/20	3/28	11/21	1/7
1/2	8/15	1/7	3/4
1/2	2/5	1/8	1/10
1/6	3/8	1/4	5/8
1/6	2/9	3/8	1/8
1/10	4/21	5/21	2/21
1/8	1/14	1/3	1/2

Page57

5/28	4/15	5/12	1/2
1/5	3/7	1/30	0
1/2	4/7	1/3	1/7
1/8	5/8	1/4	1/2
3/8	0	1/15	1/24
17/28	1/9	1/2	2/7
5/18	1/4	1/12	1/8
1/15	1/5	2/7	1/5
1/5	3/5	0	1/3
7/12	1/4	3/16	9/20

Page58

5/81	35/128	6/49	15/64
3/32	1/8	4/25	14/75
5/36	2/5	1/12	9/16
1/8	7/25	32/81	21/32
9/28	4/15	2/7	1/24
3/8	1/12	1/8	1/18
1/50	5/49	7/25	1/32
8/49	5/98	2/15	1/9
1/16	9/50	30/49	3/8
5/18	7/100	3/16	4/25

Page59

10/81	4/9	1/32	9/14
35/64	15/32	3/64	7/50
32/75	3/16	9/49	5/12
5/54	1/3	12/49	21/32
7/72	8/81	6/49	3/14
3/16	3/49	3/8	2/225
2/9	7/16	35/64	3/16
9/20	4/15	1/4	4/75
12/25	4/75	1/18	4/15
1/3	5/64	14/27	21/64

Page60

15/64	1/5	2/25	9/16
8/75	27/56	1/30	8/25
4/25	5/32	1/14	1/9
1/18	1/6	1/8	1/7
9/100	7/32	8/27	5/16
4/25	9/100	1/16	1/8
8/49	5/49	1/12	21/64
24/49	1/12	35/108	5/36
35/64	3/25	10/49	4/45
1/9	12/25	3/28	5/18

Page61

1/2	5/6	7/4	1
5/4	1/2	1/2	1/2
1/2	1/3	2	2
2	2	2	3
5/4	2	4	1
2	1/3	2/5	9/4
1/3	4/9	1	15/16
2	10/7	21/20	1/3
3/10	20/3	6/5	6/5
5/16	4/3	1	2

Page62

1	1/3	3/10	2
3/2	16/5	1/6	3/4
15/2	1	9/7	7/6
7/10	1/2	9/4	1/4
1/5	3/2	3/2	7/2
3	5/6	4/5	8/15
1/6	9/10	4/7	1/3
8/7	9/8	4/15	4/7
1/8	1/7	3/2	4/3
2/3	8/7	3/8	4

Page63

2/5	4/5	1	5/6
12/7	10/9	4	7/6
14/9	5/6	3	7/3
2/3	4/3	10	1/3
6	3/2	6	9/7
1/3	1/3	2/3	5/6
7	2	4/3	1/4
2/5	15/4	1/2	3
6	4/5	6	5/6
5/6	2/5	4/7	2/3

	1	2	3	4	5	6	7	8	9	10
page 64	30	4	8	3:03	28	750	20	252	1	10
page 65	7	34	5	52	16	18	27	1	12	56
page 66	7	24	27	6	36	8	2:30	600	29	7
page 67	1	4	11	6	16	12:40	120	65	13	4
page 68	14	32	12	8	15	8	2:02	1:40	2.75	2
page 69	5	10	12:40	75	63	18	16	4	27	41
page 70	7	25	34	15	6	2:45	8	12:40	3.96	5
page 71	33	$13.63	4.45	17.38	42	$462.28	494	5	84 1/2	1 1/2
page 72	$15.77	6.61	15	21.6	92	$159.60	1/40	348	27	34
page 73	$18.62	16	$825.00	24	132	1/5	531	9	$10.60	13
page 74	33	13.45	$100.00	15.66	604	9	4	35	$2.50	28
page 75	154	16	$800.00	468	10	18	84.5	3	12:35	$250.25

MULTIPLICATION TABLE

1 × 1 = 1	1 × 2 = 2	1 × 3 = 3	1 × 4 = 4
2 × 1 = 2	2 × 2 = 4	2 × 3 = 6	2 × 4 = 8
3 × 1 = 3	3 × 2 = 6	3 × 3 = 9	3 × 4 = 12
4 × 1 = 4	4 × 2 = 8	4 × 3 = 12	4 × 4 = 16
5 × 1 = 5	5 × 2 = 10	5 × 3 = 15	5 × 4 = 20
6 × 1 = 6	6 × 2 = 12	6 × 3 = 18	6 × 4 = 24
7 × 1 = 7	7 × 2 = 14	7 × 3 = 21	7 × 4 = 28
8 × 1 = 8	8 × 2 = 16	8 × 3 = 24	8 × 4 = 32
9 × 1 = 9	9 × 2 = 18	9 × 3 = 27	9 × 4 = 36
10 × 1 = 10	10 × 2 = 20	10 × 3 = 30	10 × 4 = 40
11 × 1 = 11	11 × 2 = 22	11 × 3 = 33	11 × 4 = 44
12 × 1 = 12	12 × 2 = 24	12 × 3 = 36	12 × 4 = 46

1 × 5 = 5	1 × 6 = 6	1 × 7 = 7	1 × 8 = 8
2 × 5 = 10	2 × 6 = 12	2 × 7 = 14	2 × 8 = 16
3 × 5 = 15	3 × 6 = 18	3 × 7 = 21	3 × 8 = 24
4 × 5 = 20	4 × 6 = 24	4 × 7 = 28	4 × 8 = 32
5 × 5 = 25	5 × 6 = 30	5 × 7 = 35	5 × 8 = 40
6 × 5 = 30	6 × 6 = 36	6 × 7 = 42	6 × 8 = 48
7 × 5 = 35	7 × 6 = 42	7 × 7 = 49	7 × 8 = 56
8 × 5 = 40	8 × 6 = 48	8 × 7 = 56	8 × 8 = 64
9 × 5 = 45	9 × 6 = 54	9 × 7 = 63	9 × 8 = 72
10 × 5 = 50	10 × 6 = 60	10 × 7 = 70	10 × 8 = 80
11 × 5 = 55	11 × 6 = 66	11 × 7 = 77	11 × 8 = 88
12 × 5 = 60	12 × 6 = 72	12 × 7 = 84	12 × 8 = 96

1 × 9 = 9	1 × 10 = 10	1 × 11 = 11	1 × 12 = 12
2 × 9 = 18	2 × 10 = 20	2 × 11 = 22	2 × 12 = 24
3 × 9 = 27	3 × 10 = 30	3 × 11 = 33	3 × 12 = 36
4 × 9 = 36	4 × 10 = 40	4 × 11 = 44	4 × 12 = 48
5 × 9 = 45	5 × 10 = 50	5 × 11 = 55	5 × 12 = 60
6 × 9 = 54	6 × 10 = 60	6 × 11 = 66	6 × 12 = 72
7 × 9 = 63	7 × 10 = 70	7 × 11 = 77	7 × 12 = 84
8 × 9 = 72	8 × 10 = 80	8 × 11 = 88	8 × 12 = 96
9 × 9 = 81	9 × 10 = 90	9 × 11 = 99	9 × 12 = 108
10 × 9 = 90	10 × 10 = 100	10 × 11 = 110	10 × 12 = 120
11 × 9 = 99	11 × 10 = 110	11 × 11 = 121	11 × 12 = 132
12 × 9 = 108	12 × 10 = 120	12 × 11 = 132	12 × 12 = 144

We appreciate your purchase. If you enjoyed reading this book, I kindly request that you take a moment to leave us a review. Your feedback is invaluable to us and greatly aids in our efforts to connect with a wider audience. Thank you for your support. Ensuring quality is a top priority for us.

Manufactured by Amazon.ca
Acheson, AB